SINGER

MAGIC FUSIBLES

IN FASHION SEWING

SINGER

MAGIC FUSIBLES
IN FASHION SEWING

Jessie Hutton

Book design, art direction,
and production supervision
Claire F. Valentine

GOLDEN PRESS • NEW YORK
Western Publishing Company, Inc.,
Racine, Wisconsin

CONTENTS

FUSIBLES IN FASHION DRESSMAKING

FUSIBLES IN FASHION TAILORING

A Note To The Reader

When iron-on and press-on sewing products were first introduced, they gave such poor results that careful sewers, myself included, were understandably skeptical about the fusible interfacings and webbing as they became available. Then, almost by accident, my skepticism dissolved into enthusiasm!

I was making a tailored garment of synthetic suede, a new and beautiful washable fabric that does not respond to conventional sewing methods. Seam allowances would not stay pressed open; they had to be held open. Interfacing was needed for the collar, facings, and hems, but hand padding stitches could not be used because this suedelike fabric is almost impossible to penetrate with a hand sewing needle.

As a last resort, I decided to try the new fusible products. They worked like magic!

Not only did fusible webbing hold the seam allowances open, but it also solved the problem of attaching the lining hem and other lining parts that had to be fitted. I was able to apply the fusible interfacing without a hitch (or even a hand stitch) wherever it was needed.

My success with synthetic suede led to still more trials and successes, and I became convinced that all women who sew could benefit from the knowledge that I had accumulated about how and where to use these new fusibles.

The information in this book is practical and useful; it is the result of extensive investigation and experimentation. My purpose is not to promote the sale of fusible products, but rather to share with you new methods of construction that will enable you to achieve professional results in your fashion sewing.

Jessie Hutton

KEY TO TEXTURES AND COLOR TINTS IN ILLUSTRATIONS

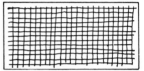

press
cloth

lightweight and
medium-weight,
nonwoven, fusible
interfacing

fashion fabric—
right side

lining fabric—
wrong side

edge of ironing
board or ironing
board cover

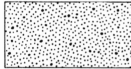

wrong side of
fusible interfacing

fashion fabric—
wrong side

underlining—
right and
wrong sides

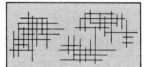

heavyweight,
woven, fusible
interfacing

fusible
webbing

lining fabric—
right side

zippers

INTRODUCING THE

fusibles

Fusible products are bringing a new dimension to fashion sewing. By applying heat, moisture, and pressure with your own steam iron, you can cause two layers of fabric to adhere to each other permanently! More than just a substitute for hand or machine stitching, fusible materials help you to produce results that are unique in fashion sewing.

In some applications, fusible materials speed up sewing construction; in others, they make possible a better-looking finished garment; and in still others, they make it possible to sew with fabrics that would not otherwise work up into attractive garments.

Fusible materials can be used by anyone who has at least a basic knowledge of sewing. Those who prefer pressing instead of hand-finishing will delight in the ease with which an interfacing, a hem, a zipper, or a facing can be fused in place.

Those who enjoy searching out and using unusual fabrics will find that with the help of fusible materials, the new suedelike, silklike, and leatherlike fabrics can easily be made into custom clothes even though they do not lend themselves readily to hand stitching.

Perhaps most important of all, fusible materials are compatible with the middle range of fabrics, knit or woven with man-made fibers, such as nylon, polyester, acrylic and their many blends.

The methods for applying fusible interfacing and webbing were developed for this book with the products listed on the charts on pages 2, 4, and 6.

It is likely that similar products will appear on the market in the future, so if you should choose a product that is not listed on the charts, be sure to test it thoroughly, using scraps of the same fabric that you intend to use for your garment.

BASIC FACTS OF FUSIBLE PRODUCTS

Different types. Fusible products are available in two distinctly different types: as webbing, and as interfacing fabric that has a fusible coating applied to one side by the manufacturer. The fusible substance in both types is usually polyamide resin, which is a form of nylon. When heat, steam, and pressure are applied, polyamide melts. When it is allowed to cool, it again returns to a solid state.

Steam pressing. When polyamide in the form of fusible webbing is placed between two layers of fabric, and heat, steam, and pressure are applied with a steam iron, the fabric layers will be fused together firmly enough to withstand normal laundry or dry-cleaning procedures.

Fusible interfacing already has a coating of polyamide applied to one side by the manufacturer. Because of this, when polyamide is fused by the heat, steam, and pressure of a steam iron, the layer of interfacing will adhere to a layer of any fabric that is compatible with the fusing process.

All fabrics are not compatible with fusibles. Fusible interfacing or webbing can be used with all fabrics that can be steam-pressed. They should *not* be used with fabrics that will water-spot, pucker, or shine if they are steam-pressed; nor used with pile or glossy-surfaced fabrics, or fabrics whose fibers will be damaged by the amount of heat recommended for fusing.

Natural leather, natural suede, and vinyl-coated fabrics not only will not tolerate the heat and steam required for fusing, but the steam and fusible material will not penetrate sufficiently below the surface of these fabrics to fuse seam allowances or hems in place.

Fabrics that have been treated to repel soil and water usually cannot be used with fusible materials. The treated surfaces resist the penetration of the steam and the fusible material so that it cannot reach the fibers of the fabric during the fusing process, resulting in poor adhesion of the fabric layers.

Triacetate, one of the most popular fabrics for wearing apparel, cannot be used readily with fusible products because the fusible resin will not adhere to triacetate fibers. However, in triacetate collars, cuffs, and lapels, fusible interfacing can be used if it is first lightly fused, and then stitched into the seams and along the facing edges.

Rayon or any fabric for which low iron temperatures are specified should not be used with fusible products because they will not tolerate the amount of heat needed for fusing. Read the fabric labels carefully for fiber content and care information as a guide to iron temperatures and moisture tolerance, but make it a practice to test the fusible product on scraps of fabric before you apply it to the garment fabric that you are planning to use.

Fusible Interfacings

In recent years the demand for polyester double knits in women's and men's clothes has helped to accelerate the development of the technology related to fusible interfacings. The traditional padding stitches, whether done by hand or by factory machines, dimpled the fabric, and because synthetic yarns resist the penetration of a needle, hand sewing was more difficult to do on suit-weight double knits than on fabrics woven of natural fibers. As a result of this research, today's home sewer has a wide choice of fusible interfacings that are compatible with a great variety of knit and woven fabrics.

The newest fusible interfacings use polyamide resin as the adhesive, which requires heat, steam, and pressure to fuse. Iron-on interfacings that require heat only are usually not coated with polyamide resin. Manufacturers cleverly have applied just enough fusible coating to hold the interfacing in position, but not enough to make the garment rigid or harsh-looking.

Generally, except for a few specific situations, it is better to use fusible interfacing than a layer of plain interfacing plus a layer of fusible webbing because the fusible interfacing transfers less resin into the fabric than does the webbing, and does not change the hand of the fabric. However, there are a few instances

FUSIBLE INTERFACING CHART

COMPANY	PRODUCT NAME	CONSTRUCTION	WEIGHT/RECOMMENDED USES
The Armo[1][†] Company Division of Crown Textile Mfg. Corporation 206 W. 40th St. New York, N.Y. 10018	Fusible P-91	Woven.	Lightweight iron-on interfacing for shaping small detail areas in light- to-medium-weig knit and woven fabrics.
	Fusible Acro (Silver metallic selvage stripe)	Woven.	All-purpose interfacing for jacket and coat fronts and collars in medium- to heavyweig polyester knits, woolens and wool blends. Underlining for coats and suits.
	Fusible Formite (Gold metallic selvage stripe)	Woven (napped surface).	Sheer interfacing for jacket and shirt fronts cuffs, hems, yokes, pocket flaps and welts buttonholes, and plackets in light- to-medi weight knit and woven fabrics.
	Stylus™ Detail fusible	Nonwoven.	For small detail area reinforcement; for crafts and decorating; for backing pattern pieces.
	Stylus™ Fusible Uni-Stretch™ Light Weight	Nonwoven. Lengthwise stability; crosswise stretch.	For soft natural shaping of light- to-mediu weight knit and woven fabrics in all interfacing and reinforcement areas
	Stylus™ Fusible Uni-Stretch™ Suit Weight	Nonwoven. Lengthwise stability; crosswise stretch.	For natural shaping in tailoring medium-to-heavyweight knit and woven fabrics in all interfacing areas.

[†]Numbers indicate owners of registered or trademark names, as shown on page 5.

where you may prefer to use webbing plus plain interfacing, such as in the collar of a suit jacket where you could fuse the interfacing only to the stand portion of the under collar. In the jacket front you could fuse the interfacing to the lapel portion only.

There are some recent developments that have made fusible products suitable for fluid fashions, such as fusible nonwoven interfacings that give crosswise, but are stable lengthwise; and fusible nylon tricot interfacings that also can serve as a lining or as a facing.

Refer to the fusible interfacing chart below and on pages 4 and 5 to familiarize yourself with the brand names, interfacing characteristics, and the care and use recommendations of the manufacturers.

Fabric Care Labeling

To inform consumers about the proper care of fabrics, the Federal Trade Commission in 1972 passed a regulation requiring that all fabrics manufactured and sold as piece goods be accompanied by a care method label. Sometimes only a number enclosed in a triangle is used to indicate the proper care method for the fabric.

The list that follows shows the care method that has been assigned to each number.

1 • Machine wash, warm.
2 • Machine wash, warm; line dry.
3 • Machine wash, warm, tumble dry; remove promptly.
4 • Machine wash, warm, delicate cycle; tumble dry, low; cool iron.
5 • Machine wash, warm; do not dry-clean.
6 • Hand wash separately; use cool iron.
7 • Dry-clean only.
8 • Dry-clean; pile fabric method only.
9 • Wipe with damp cloth only.

ER CONTENT	WIDTH	COLORS	CARE	SPECIAL INSTRUCTIONS
100% cotton	22" 38" 45"	Black White	Machine wash on warm, delicate cycle. Tumble dry on low heat. Use cool iron. Dry-cleanable. CARE METHOD △4	Use damp press cloth. Set iron at "Permanent Press." Steam-press for 7 seconds.
70% rayon 21% polyester 9% goat hair	25"	White	Shrinkage controlled. Machine wash on warm, delicate cycle. Tumble dry on low heat. Use cool iron. Dry-cleanable. CARE METHOD △4	Use damp press cloth. Set iron at "Permanent Press." Steam-press firmly for 10 seconds. (Do not slide iron.)
50% rayon 50% cotton	23"	Natural White	Shrinkage controlled. Machine wash on warm, delicate cycle. Tumble dry on low heat. Use cool iron. Dry-cleanable. CARE METHOD △4	Use damp press cloth. Set iron at "Permanent Press." Steam-press firmly for 7 seconds. (Do not slide iron.)
100% rayon	22"	White	Preshrunk. Machine wash on warm cycle. Dry-cleanable. CARE METHOD △1	Use wet press cloth. Set iron at "Wool." Steam-press for 10–12 seconds.
70% nylon 20% polyester 10% rayon 100% polyamide fusible dot	25" 36"	White Charcoal	Preshrunk. Machine wash on warm cycle. Dry-cleanable. CARE METHOD △1	Use lightweight, wet press cloth. Set iron at "Wool." Steam-press firmly for 10–12 seconds. Check adhesion after fabric has cooled. If necessary, turn fabric over and repeat the process on right side.

(Continued on pages 4 and 5)

COMPANY	PRODUCT NAME	CONSTRUCTION	WEIGHT/RECOMMENDED USES
The Armo[1†] Company	FuseAKnit™	Tricot knit. Same lengthwise stability as tricot knit; same crosswise stretch as tricot knit.	For soft, flexible fusible interfacing and fusible underlining of knit and woven fabric. Also can be used as a facing for armholes, neckline openings, sleeve plackets, and hems.
Pellon[2] Corporation 1120 Avenue of the Americas New York, N.Y. 10036	Tri-Dimensional® Computer Dot® Midweight Fusible Pellon®	Nonwoven. Stabilized lengthwise; gives crosswise.	Professionally shapes medium- to-heavy-weight knit and woven fabrics. **Not recommended** for triacetates, pure silks, and silklike wovens, lightweight sheer lightweight cotton-blend wovens; fabrics with soil, stain, or water repellent finishes or fabrics that cannot be steam-pressed.
	All-Bias Computer Dot® Featherweight Fusible Pellon®	Nonwoven. All-Bias, has give in all directions.	Allows gentle control and shaping for facing collars, cuffs, detail areas in construction of shirts, blouses, dresses, sportswear. Cut in any direction.
Stacy[3] Fabrics Corporation 469 Seventh Avenue New York, N.Y. 10018	Shape-Flex® Nonwoven	Nonwoven.	For small detail areas and crafts.
	Shape-Flex® All-Purpose	Woven.	Soft and supple, for large or small areas.
	Suit-Shape®	Woven (napped surface).	Canvas interfacing for easy tailoring on medium- to-heavyweight fabrics.
	Easy-Shaper® Light Weight	Nonwoven. Stabilized lengthwise; gives crosswise.	Soft and supple fabrics. In dress or shirtweight fabrics.
	Easy-Shaper® Suit Weight	Nonwoven. Stabilized lengthwise; gives crosswise.	Relaxed and flexible, for interfacing men's or women's suits, jackets, and dresses.
Colton/Glendale[4] J. P. Stevens & Company, Inc. 1185 Avenue of the Americas New York, N.Y. 10036	Kyron 4010®	Nonwoven. Stabilized lengthwise; gives crosswise.	Lightweight. For soft, natural shaping of light- to medium-weight knit and woven fabrics in all interfacing and reinforcement areas.
	Kyron 5001®	Nonwoven. Stabilized lengthwise; gives crosswise.	Medium weight. Allows gentle control and shaping for facings, collars, cuffs, detail areas in construction of shirts, blouses, dresses, sportswear. Cut in any direction.

†Numbers indicate owners of registered or trademark names, as shown on page 5.

BER CONTENT	WIDTH	COLORS	CARE	SPECIAL INSTRUCTIONS
ylon plus fusing gent	22" 45"	Beige White Gray Black	Preshrunk. Machine wash on warm cycle. Tumble dry. Dry-cleanable. CARE METHOD △3	Use lightweight *dry* press cloth. Set iron at "Permanent Press." Steam-press firmly for 10–12 seconds. (Do not slide iron.)
end of 0% polyester 0% nylon 00% polyamide sing dot	21"	White Gray	Preshrunk. Machine wash on warm cycle. Dry-cleanable. CARE METHOD △1	Use muslin-weight, wet press cloth. Set iron no lower than "Wool." Steam-press firmly for 10–15 seconds. For heavyweight fabrics, steam-press on right side also, to ensure complete fusing.
0% viscose 0% polyester 00% polyamide sing dot	22"	White Gray	Preshrunk. Machine wash on warm cycle. Dry-cleanable. CARE METHOD △1	Use lightweight, wet press cloth. Set iron at "Permanent Press." Steam-press firmly for 10 seconds. Steam-press again on right side.
00% rayon	18"	Black White	Machine wash on warm cycle. Dry-cleanable. CARE METHOD △1	Apply with dry iron set at "Wool." Press firmly for 10 seconds.
00% cotton	18"	Black White	Machine wash on warm cycle. Dry-cleanable. CARE METHOD △1	
0% cotton 0% rayon	22"	Natural White	Preshrunk. Machine wash on warm cycle. Dry-cleanable. CARE METHOD △1	Use damp press cloth. Set iron at "Wool." Steam-press firmly for 10 seconds. (Do not slide iron.)
0% nylon 0% polyester 0% rayon 00% polyamide sin	25"	White Charcoal	Preshrunk. Machine wash on warm cycle. Dry-cleanable. CARE METHOD △1	Use damp press cloth. Set iron on "Wool." Steam-press firmly for 10 seconds. Check adhesion after fabric has cooled. If necessary, turn fabric over and repeat the process on right side. With dry iron use wet press cloth.
	25"	White Charcoal	Preshrunk. Machine wash on warm cycle. Dry-cleanable. CARE METHOD △1	
00% polyester	25"	White Charcoal	Preshrunk. Machine wash on warm cycle. Dry-cleanable. CARE METHOD △1	Use damp press cloth. Set iron on "Wool." Steam-press firmly for 10 seconds. Check adhesion after fabric has cooled. If necessary, turn fabric over and repeat the process on right side.
00% polyester	25"	White Charcoal	Preshrunk. Machine wash on warm cycle. Tumble dry. Dry-cleanable. CARE METHOD △3	

[1]The Armo Company
[2]Pellon Corporation
[3]Stacy Fabrics Corporation
[4]J. P. Stevens & Co., Inc.
[5]Coats and Clark Sales Corp.

Fusible Webbing

Fusible webbing can be purchased either by the yard or in packaged strips, rolls, and sheets. (See chart below.)

Webbing yardage is available wherever interfacings are sold, and it comes in 10-, 18-, and 21-inch widths depending on which brand you select. All manufacturers provide printed plastic interleaves with instructions and suggestions for using their products in dressmaking, in various crafts, and for decorating. The interleaves serve to keep the fusible layers separated until the webbing is used; they are cut with the yardage and given to the customer as part of her purchase.

Packaged strips, rolls, and sheets of webbing are available at notion counters of department, fabric, and variety stores. Although all brands are made of polyamide, their appearance and density vary slightly from one brand to another, so try the different brands to see which one you prefer. Whether you use precut strips or yardage, the results will be exactly the same; the difference between the two types is only a matter of convenience or of saving cutting time.

Fusible webbing has extraordinary versatility: it can be pinned, cut to the shape of a pattern piece, marked either with a pencil or a tracing wheel and tracing paper, stitched permanently by hand or by machine, and spot-fused instead of basted for temporary positioning.

Although fusible webbing is appropriate for both knit and woven fabrics, it is particularly suited to knits because it gives with the fabric, letting it breathe, stretch, and recover in its natural way. In woven fabrics it prevents the cut yarns from raveling because they are fused together, and the webbing eliminates puckers in the seams.

FUSIBLE WEBBING CHART			
COMPANY	**NAME**	**FORM**	**COMMENTS**
The Armo[1][†] Company Division of Crown Textile Mfg. Corporation 206 W. 40th St. New York, N.Y. 10018	Stylus ™ Fusible Web	By the yard: 18″ wide	100% polyamide. Washable and dry-cleanable. Instructions are printed on plastic interleaves, cut with the yardage when purchased.
Coats & Clark[5] Sales Corporation 72 Cummings Pt. Rd. Stamford, Conn. 06902	Polyweb®	Packaged: ¾″ x 3½ yds. 2″ x 3 yds. 9″ x 18″ 9″ x 36″ Rolls: ¾″ x 15 yds. 2″ x 10 yds.	100% polyamide. Washable and dry-cleanable. Instructions are printed on package.
Pellon[2] Corporation 1120 Avenue of the Americas New York, N.Y. 10036	Pellon® Fusible Web	By the yard: 21″ wide	100% polyamide. Washable and dry-cleanable. Instructions are printed on plastic interleaves, cut with the yardage when purchased.
Stacy[3] Fabrics Corporation 469 Seventh Avenue New York, N.Y. 10018	Stitch Witchery™	By the yard: 18″ wide 10″ wide Packaged: ¾″ x 12 yds.	100% polyamide. Washable and dry-cleanable. Instructions are printed on plastic interleaves, cut with the yardage when purchased. Packaged hem tape includes instructions.

[†]Numbers indicate owners of registered or trademark names, as shown on page 5.

PREPARATIONS FOR FUSING AN INTERFACING

The care with which you prepare your fashion fabric, the garment sections, and the fusible interfacing before you begin the fusing process will influence the quality of your garment for better or for worse.

Fashion Fabric

All fabric must be shrunk before it is cut, but this is especially true if you are planning to use fusible interfacing. The fabric label or information on the bolt will let you know whether the fabric is preshrunk; if it is not preshrunk, you will have to shrink it yourself. The fabric care label will indicate which shrinking method to use. Fabrics that can be laundered should be laundered before they are cut, using the same method that you will use throughout the life of the garment. Fabrics that are labeled "⚠ Dry-clean only" should be sent to a tailor or dry cleaner for steam-pressing.

The shrink-before-cutting requirement is common to all good sewing methods; it is not a special rule that applies only when you use fusible interfacing. However, should you forget to shrink your fabric before cutting it, you may notice puckers between the fused and unfused areas of a garment section. The puckers occur because the fused part of a garment section will shrink more than the unfused part. It is the steam-pressing, not the fusible product, that causes the shrinkage.

To prepare the fashion fabric properly for cutting, straighten and square the crosswise grain before shrinking. After the fabric has been shrunk, *press* the fabric before laying it out for pattern placement. Then, following the pattern guide sheet, place the pattern pieces on the straight grain of the fabric according to the pattern grain-line markings. These preparations will ensure that the completed garment will fit and hang properly.

Garment Sections

After the garment sections have been cut from the fabric, separate the ones to which interfacing will be fused from the others. Transfer all pattern markings to the garment sections except to those parts of the sections that will be covered with fusible interfacing; there the pattern markings should be transferred to the interfacing. Do not remove the paper pattern from any

section until you are ready to work with that section because the pinned-on pattern piece will prevent storage wrinkles in the fabric.

Just before you are ready to fuse interfacing to a garment section, lay the section on the ironing board with the wrong side up, and steam-press the entire section. Do not let any part hang over the edge of the ironing board; it will stretch and distort the shape of the section.

Whenever you are working with right and left sections, place them side by side with their wrong sides up so that you will really have a pair of sections and not duplicates. Duplicates result when interfacing is fused to the wrong side of one section and fused to the right side of the other section. This is more likely to happen on small sections such as cuffs, pocket flaps, and pockets than on jacket fronts with lapels.

Fusible Interfacing

Fusible interfacing cannot be pressed before it is cut because of its sensitivity to heat. To avoid wrinkles and sharp creases, handle and store it carefully with the plastic interleaf that comes with it.

Woven, fusible interfacing usually has grain lines that are true, that is, their lengthwise and crosswise yarns are perpendicular to each other. If you should happen to buy yardage that is not true, straighten it by cutting along the track of a drawn crosswise yarn at each end of the yardage, and pull the yardage diagonally to square the yarns. Always smooth the yardage on a table with your hands only; *never use an iron!*

Nonwoven, fusible interfacing is available in two types; stabilized lengthwise and all-bias.

The *stabilized lengthwise* type gives freely in the crosswise direction, but is completely stable in the lengthwise direction. Cut this interfacing according to the lengthwise grain markings of the pattern except where the manufacturer's instructions differ from standard sewing practice. An example of conflicting instructions occurs where the under-collar pattern of a jacket or suit is marked for bias cutting of regular, woven interfacing, and the manufacturer's instructions suggest that the center back seam be placed on the lengthwise grain of the fusible interfacing.

The *all-bias* type of fusible interfacing has no direc-

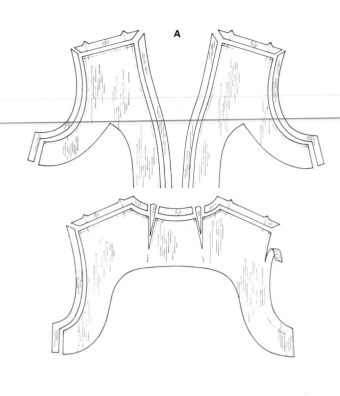

A

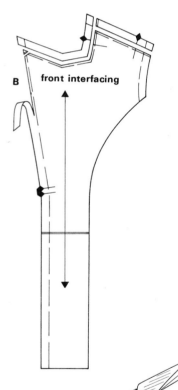

B

front interfacing

C

D

tion, allowing pattern sections to be placed at any angle without regard for the pattern's directional markings.

When cutting two layers of fusible interfacing, lay it with the fusible sides together, and position and pin the pattern sections to the interfacing just as carefully as you would if you were preparing to cut your fashion fabric. Be especially careful to lay the fold line of the pattern precisely on the interfacing fold to prevent cutting an interfacing section that could be either too large or too small.

Fusible interfacing should extend $\frac{1}{8}$ inch into all seam and dart allowances in most instances. There are several ways you can do this:

1. Cut the interfacing with $\frac{5}{8}$-inch seam allowances, the same as the pattern, and trim off $\frac{1}{2}$ inch before fusing, leaving $\frac{1}{8}$ inch to extend into each seam and dart allowance [A].

2. Using either the interfacing pattern piece or a specially cut interfacing pattern, trim $\frac{1}{2}$ inch from all seam allowances, and wherever there are darts, trim the center from each dart, leaving $\frac{1}{8}$ inch to extend into each seam and dart allowance [B]. Then cut the interfacing by the specially prepared pattern.

3. Cut the interfacing with $\frac{5}{8}$-inch seam allowances by the regular pattern. Mark the seam and dart lines with a tracing wheel and tracing paper. Trim the dart allowances $\frac{1}{8}$ inch from the stitching lines, but do not trim the seam allowances yet. Instead, lightly fuse the interfacing to each section. Stitch the sections together and before crossing seams, trim the interfacing seam allowances $\frac{1}{8}$ inch outside the stitching, as on shoulder seam shown [C]. With your fingertips, loosen the interfacing that covers the seam allowances [D], and trim off the interfacing $\frac{1}{8}$ inch outside the stitching. ***Steam-press to fuse*** the interfacing to the garment section firmly. Refer to pages 10 and 11.

EQUIPMENT NEEDED FOR FUSING

If you already do a reasonable amount of sewing, it is more than likely that you have at hand all the equipment that is needed for fusing, such as an ironing board to use as a padded fusing surface; press cloths in various sizes, and a steam iron that heats evenly.

Fusing Surface

The surface of a smoothly padded ironing board is usually large enough to accommodate most garment sections for fusing interfacing. *Do not* let any areas of a garment section hang over the edge of the ironing board; they may either stretch or distort other parts of the garment section.

For areas that are too large to fuse on an ironing board, substitute a counter top, a table, or a hard-surfaced floor. Protect the surfaces of these substitute ironing boards from the steam and heat with a thick layer of newspaper, a cardboard cutting board, or a bed board; then pad with layers of soft fabric, such as sheets, towels, or a bedspread. For the top layer, cover the surface with muslin or an old sheet.

A sleeve board, press mitt, tailor's ham, and a seam board are useful for applying fusible webbing to small areas during garment construction.

Press Cloths

It is essential that you have several press cloths at hand for fusing interfacing and webbing. Alone, the steam from the iron is not sufficient to fuse polyamide resin, and additional steam must be produced from the moisture in the press cloth. A soft, thirsty, porous cotton fabric that will absorb water evenly, and can be squeezed dry enough not to drip, makes the best press cloths. Use such fabrics as all-cotton muslin, batiste, closely woven cheesecloth, and similar smooth, all-cotton fabrics. *Do not* use cotton blends, especially no-iron sheets; they do not absorb water evenly, and when they are used as press cloths for fusing, the garment fabric will be wet instead of steamed. Packaged all-purpose cheesecloth is too loosely woven for fusing, but if you decide to use it, stitch at least four layers together.

You should have several sizes of press cloths: long, narrow ones for fusing seam allowances; small ones for fusing darts, collars, and cuffs; and a large one for fusing a front and lapel section. *Do not* use press cloths that are smaller in length or width than the soleplate of the iron. Suggested sizes are illustrated at the bottom of this page.

If a press cloth accidentally becomes smeared with the fusible resin, discard the smeared part to avoid transferring the smear to the right side of your fashion fabric. It is a worthwhile precaution to use two sets of press cloths, one set for fusing and one set for pressing, so you can always be sure that you are using a clean press cloth when you are pressing the right side of the garment fabric.

Steam Iron

The steam iron that you use for fusing should have a dependable heat control, and it should heat evenly over the entire surface of the soleplate. Most instruction sheets for fusible products recommend pressing with a steam iron that is held stationary in one position for a specified number of *seconds* before the iron is lifted and placed on another area. After following this recommendation, you may find that the iron's steam vents are embossed on the interfacing when you test-fuse your fabric. *If this should occur,* instead of holding the steam iron stationary as you press to fuse, move the iron in a slow, back-and-forth rotational motion as you **steam-press to fuse** for the required number of seconds. (See charts on pages 2 to 5.) This will equalize the downward pressure of the iron over the area that is being fused, and will prevent the outlines of the vents from showing on the fabric. Remember, press; do not iron! Pressing is the action of *placing* and *lifting* the iron. Ironing is the action of *sliding* the iron in the direction of the lengthwise grain of the fabric.

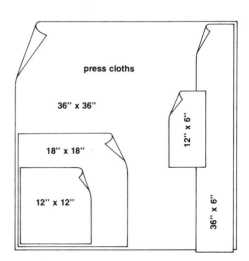

press cloths

36" x 36"

18" x 18"

12" x 12"

12" x 6"

36" x 6"

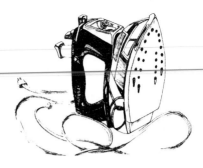

HOW TO FUSE INTERFACING AND WEBBING

"Practice makes perfect" is the watchword before you try to apply fusible interfacing or webbing to your first garment. Learning *how to fuse* is only part of the game; learn *how to spot-fuse, how to lightly fuse,* and *how to test* your fashion fabric before you use fusible interfacing or webbing with it.

Practice Fusing Interfacing

You will have a more thorough knowledge of the fusing process if you practice with several weights and types of leftover fabrics from previous sewing projects in combination with samples of various fusible interfacings purchased from yardage.

Prepare scraps of fashion fabric the same way as you would if you were going to make a garment. Square, straighten, shrink, and press them as described on page 14.

Cut interfacing to conform to two edges of each piece of fashion fabric but a little narrower than the fashion fabric. After the interfacing has been fused, you will be able to see the difference between the fused and unfused areas exactly as they would be if the interfacing had been fused to a front section. Refer to *Compatibility* on page 14.

Prepare the press cloth, and have a container of water at hand as a source of moisture.

Fill the steam iron with water, and preheat the iron at the setting recommended on the interfacing instruction sheet or on the chart on pages 3 and 5.

Press the fashion fabric on the wrong side while you have it positioned on the ironing board for fusing.

Position the interfacing with the fusible side against the wrong side of the fashion fabric. Use pins placed at random to hold the edge of the trimmed seam allowance of the interfacing at a measured $\frac{1}{2}$ inch from the fabric edge. Plunge the pins through the interfacing and fashion fabric into the ironing board cover [E]. Spot-fuse lightly between the pins; then remove the pins. Refer to *Spot-fusing Instead of Basting* on page 12.

Immerse the press cloth in water, and squeeze out as much of the water as possible. You will be able to squeeze enough water out of a soft press cloth to make it just right for fusing, but after wringing out a densely woven cloth, fold it to about the size of the soleplate of the iron, and set the hot iron on top of it for a few seconds to force the moisture to penetrate the fabric evenly.

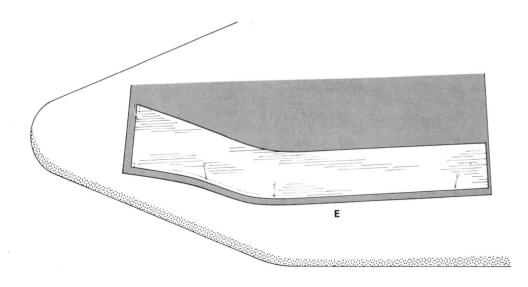

E

Cover the interfacing with the wet press cloth. For most interfacing sections of garment size, it is best to use a press cloth large enough to cover the entire area to be fused. For fusing very large areas on a counter top or other substitute fusing surface, a press cloth large enough to cover the entire area would not be practical, so immerse the press cloth again for each area to be fused.

Steam-press to fuse is a phrase that appears frequently in the text of this book. It denotes the complete procedure to be followed for fusing fabric layers together.

1. Cover the area to be fused with a damp press cloth.
2. Place a properly heated steam iron on the press cloth, and exert downward pressure without sliding the iron.
3. Count the specified number of seconds accurately for proper fusing.

How you count the seconds is unimportant, but it is vital that the fusing continue for the specified number of seconds, so either use a watch having a second hand, or count off the seconds to yourself.

After fusing the first area for the required time, lift the iron and place it on the adjoining area, slightly overlapping the first area, and start the count in seconds again. Repeat the procedure until the entire interfacing section has been fused [F]. After removing the press cloth, allow the fabric to cool and dry for a few seconds.

Test the adhesion between the two fabric layers by lifting a corner of the interfacing with your fingertips [G]. If you can still see the shape of the fusible dots or granules, the fusing is incomplete. It may be that the fabric and interfacing that you are using require more heat, more fusing time, or more moisture on the press cloth. It may be necessary to *steam-press to fuse* on the right side of the garment fabric. You will learn something about the fusing process from each combination of fabric and fusible interfacing that you try.

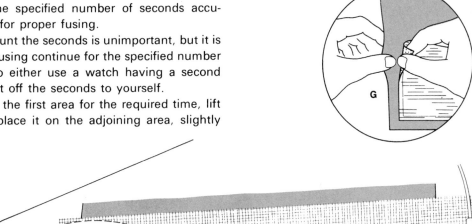

Practice Fusing Webbing

Always place fusible webbing between two layers of fabric [H], cover the top layer with a damp press cloth, and *steam-press to fuse* the same way as for fusible interfacing. Use the recommended heat setting, and count the number of seconds accurately. Hot steam must penetrate the top layer of fabric sufficiently to change the gossamerlike web of polyamide from a solid state to a liquid so that it can penetrate the fibers of the two layers of fabric. Unless this change occurs, fusing cannot take place.

At first, practice just by placing a piece of webbing between two pieces of fashion fabric with their wrong sides together, and *steam-press to fuse.* Allow the fabric to cool a little and dry before you test the adhesion by trying to pull the two layers apart [I].

To learn how various fabrics react to fusible webbing, practice on different combinations. Fuse a lining fabric to a fashion fabric; fuse two fabrics that have different textures; fuse seam allowances, following procedures described elsewhere in this book. The more you practice, the more adept at fusing you will become.

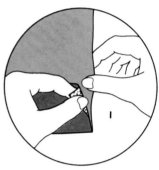

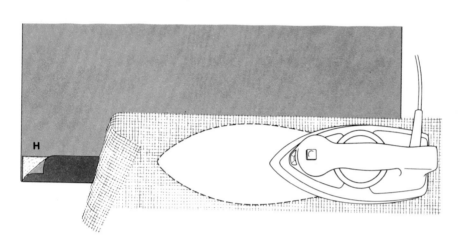

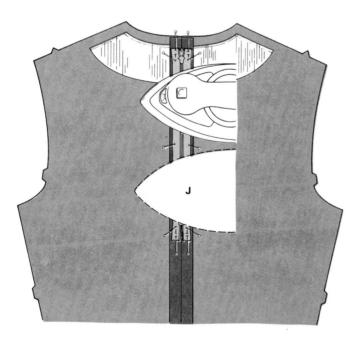

Spot-fusing Instead of Basting

Spot-fusing is a method of applying just enough heat, steam, and pressure with the tip of a steam iron to fuse the polyamide resin in enough small areas to hold the fabric layers in place until they can be fused permanently, thereby eliminating the need for basting [J].

Spot-fusing is especially appropriate to use on a garment section when pins are being used to hold fusible interfacing in place before permanent fusing, or in a zipper application when pins are being used to hold the zipper tapes in place before fusing them permanently to the seam allowances with fusible webbing.

First, spot-fuse briefly between the pins; then remove the pins, cover the entire application with a damp press cloth, and *steam-press to fuse. Do not fuse over the pins!*

Lightly Fusing Before Trimming Interfacing Seam Allowances

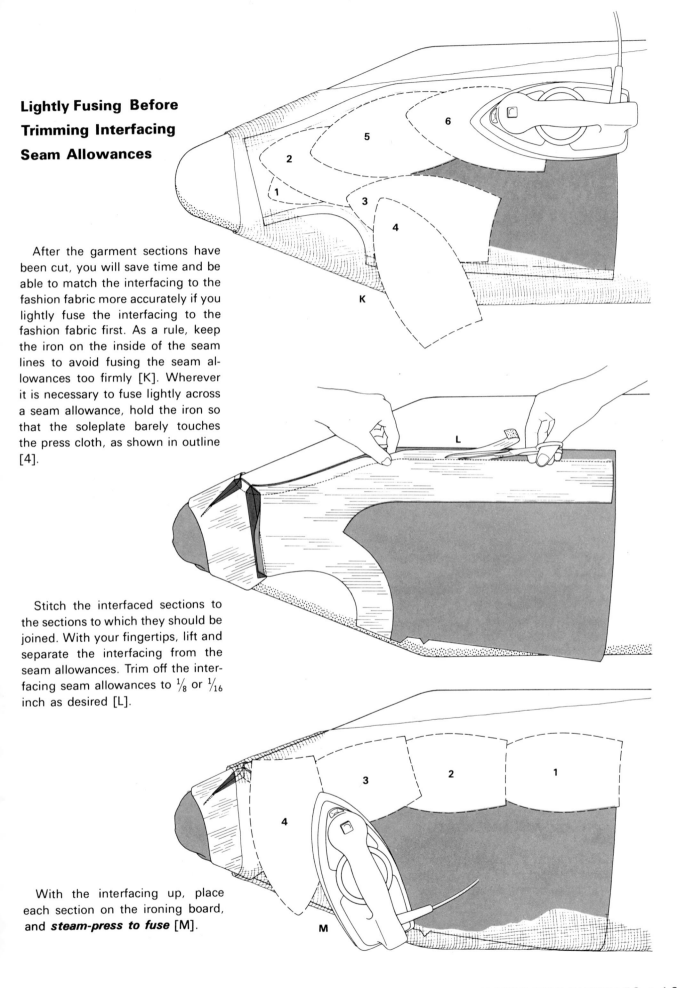

After the garment sections have been cut, you will save time and be able to match the interfacing to the fashion fabric more accurately if you lightly fuse the interfacing to the fashion fabric first. As a rule, keep the iron on the inside of the seam lines to avoid fusing the seam allowances too firmly [K]. Wherever it is necessary to fuse lightly across a seam allowance, hold the iron so that the soleplate barely touches the press cloth, as shown in outline [4].

Stitch the interfaced sections to the sections to which they should be joined. With your fingertips, lift and separate the interfacing from the seam allowances. Trim off the interfacing seam allowances to $\frac{1}{8}$ or $\frac{1}{16}$ inch as desired [L].

With the interfacing up, place each section on the ironing board, and *steam-press to fuse* [M].

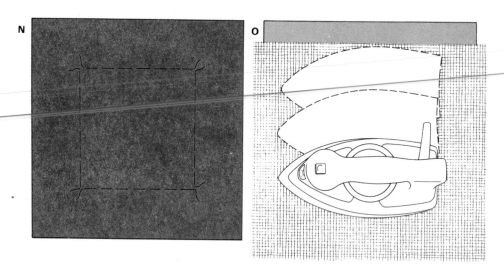

Testing Your Fashion Fabric

Before you test your fashion fabric with fusible products, it is essential that it be straightened, squared, and shrunk. Fabric that has been preshrunk by the manufacturer needs no further shrinking.

The first test should be made before the fabric has been cut because it tests the fabric for its tolerance of heat, steam, and shrinkage as well as for water-spotting, color-fading, heat damage, and similar mishaps.

The second test is for establishing the compatibility of the fusible product with the garment fabric and the fashion design.

Test for Shrinkage, Steam-and-Heat-Tolerance. For the first test, cut a swatch from the yardage, and carefully mark a 6-inch square on it with short, even, hand basting [N]. Do not knot the ends of the basting thread so that the fabric can shrink or stretch without restraint. With the wrong side up, place the marked square of fabric on the ironing board, and cover it with a wet press cloth. With the steam iron set at the specified fusing temperature, press the square of fabric, holding the iron in one position for the number of seconds specified for fusing [O].

After the fabric has cooled, measure the square carefully to find out if it has shrunk. If it shrank during the test, it will shrink also when you apply a fusible product, so use conventional interfacing instead, and use laundering or dry-cleaning methods that will subject the fabric to lower heat and less moisture than will the fusing process. In addition, inspect the steampressed area of the fabric for signs of water spots, shinyness, or changes in color that may have been caused by the heat and moisture.

Test for Compatibility. The second test is made by fusing interfacing to a scrap of your fashion fabric in the same way as described under *Practice Fusing Interfacing*, on page 10.

Make a test project that is similar to any fusing technique you are planning to use on your garment so that you may judge how a finished garment section will look beforehand. It is often a process of trial and error before you find the one fusible product that exactly fills your requirements [P].

To answer the question, to fuse or not to fuse, base your decision on the results obtained from the tests that you make yourself.

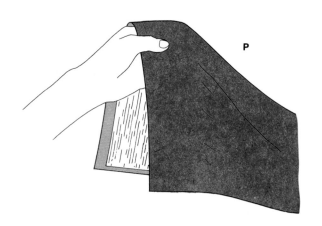

Removing Fusible Products

To remove fusible interfacing, cover the interfacing with a wet press cloth, and steam-press for ten seconds. While still warm, gently separate the interfacing from the fashion fabric. If the section is large, steampress only part of the section at one time, separating each pressed part while it is still warm as you progress from one part to the next. After the entire section has been separated, you will find that some of the fusible resin still remains on the wrong side of the fabric. To remove it, apply a wet press cloth to the wrong side of the fabric and steam-press. Repeat this procedure several times, using a fresh press cloth each time, until all the residue of the resin has been absorbed. Discard all press cloths used for this purpose as a safety precaution.

fusibles

IN SIMPLE DRESSMAKING

When an expert wants to make a smart-looking dress in the shortest period of time, she chooses a fabric that is easy to sew, then she picks a pattern that is appropriate for her fabric, and sews her garment, using the basic principles and methods of simple dressmaking.

Simple dressmaking makes it possible—for the expert as well as the beginner—to create a wardrobe of fine clothes without spending too many hours in the making. A simply styled garment can be completed much more quickly than one cut either by a complicated pattern or from a fabric that requires special handling.

Knit or woven easy-to-sew fabrics, those in the middle range in weight and texture, do not need a seam finish because they do not ravel; they do not pucker when they are stitched, nor do they require an underlining. Garments made of easy-to-sew fabrics can be worn more frequently than most because they are easy to dry-clean, launder, and press, and they are compatible with fusible products.

It is no wonder that more women, by far, do simple dressmaking than any other type of sewing!

Although fusible materials greatly speed construction in simple dressmaking, they tend to emphasize rather than conceal sewing errors. It is therefore extremely important that you have a basic knowledge of sewing before you attempt to use fusibles. Before cutting your fashion fabric, you should know how to straighten it, put it on grain, shrink and press it. You should also know how to fit your pattern as well as your garment, and how to press correctly as you stitch.

NECKLINE INTERFACINGS

If you decide to use a fusible interfacing instead of a regular interfacing for a neckline, you have to determine which type, weight, and texture to use. Each of the fusible interfacings has slightly different characteristics, but all of them work well. *Base your decision on the results of your own fabric scrap tests.*

Instead of using a manufactured fusible interfacing, you can make your own fusible interfacing by using regular interfacing, underlining, or nylon tricot fabric in conjunction with fusible webbing.

The following fusible interfacings are available and suitable for simple dressmaking:

Nonwoven
- Easy-Shaper[3][†] Light Weight by Stacy
- All-Bias Computer Dot[2] Featherweight
- Fusible Pellon[2]
- Stylus[1] Fusible Uni-Stretch Light Weight by Armo

Woven
- Fusible P-91[1] Cotton by Armo
- Shape-Flex[3] All-Purpose by Stacy

[†]Numbers indicate owners of registered or trademark names, as shown on page 5.

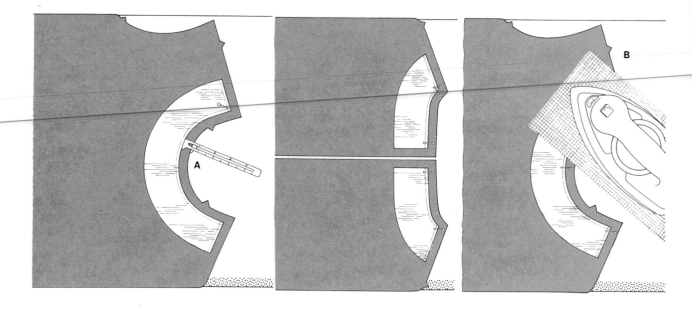

Faced Round Necklines

Preparation. Cut fusible interfacing by the facing pattern. Cut ½ inch from the neckline and shoulder seam allowances. Cut ⅝ inch from the unnotched edge and from the seam allowances where the zipper will be located. To conserve interfacing material, cut and trim a paper pattern for each interfacing section

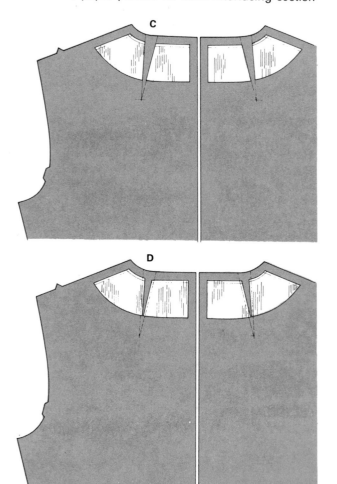

instead of trimming the interfacing after it has been cut. If the interfacing has a grain, place the pattern sections with the lengthwise arrows on the lengthwise grain. Place garment sections right side down on an ironing board, and steam-press to remove wrinkles before positioning the interfacing.

Fusing Interfacings. With the wrong side of the fabric up, place the fusible interfacing on the neckline with the fusible surface down. Measuring carefully, position the interfacing so that there is ½ inch between the neckline seam edge and the edge of the interfacing [A], with the interfacing ½ inch from the shoulder seam edges. Pin the interfacing at the neckline center front and at each shoulder. Using a damp cloth for a *press-on* fusible interfacing, or a dry cloth for an *iron-on* fusible interfacing, follow the product directions, and spot-fuse between the pins to bond the interfacing in place [B]. Remove the pins, and **steam-press to fuse.**

Darts in back neckline. With a tracing wheel and tracing paper, mark the dart stitching lines on the fashion fabric and on the interfacing [C]. Cut the interfacing on the dart stitching lines. Position each interfacing section accurately, and hold it in place with pins. Spot-fuse between the pins, then remove the pins, and **steam-press to fuse.**

Another method is to cut the interfacing ⅛ inch outside the dart stitching lines, allowing the interfacing to extend ⅛ inch into the dart allowances [D]. While this method adds more firmness to the interfaced area, the regular method is usually preferred on dresses.

Fusible Webbing Plus Interfacing

Use a lightweight, nonwoven interfacing plus fusible webbing instead of fusible interfacing. Cut the webbing and interfacing identically; then follow the same steps as described above for the method that uses fusible interfacing. Insert the webbing between the wrong side of the fashion fabric and the interfacing. First, spot-fuse; then **steam-press to fuse.**

Faced Square, V- and U-shaped Necklines

For faced square or U-shaped necklines, cut and trim fusible interfacing by the facing pattern as described for a round faced neckline.

For a V-neckline, cut the front interfacing with the lengthwise grain parallel to the neckline seam line to prevent the bias neckline seam from stretching [E]. Abut the ends of the interfacing at the center-front fold. If the pattern has a seam at the center front, allow the interfacing to extend $\frac{1}{8}$ inch into the seam allowances. Fusible interfacing eliminates the need for stay stitching and further reinforcement of the inside corners.

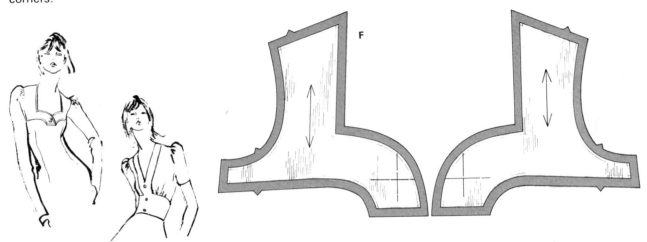

Neckline and Yoke Section

For any neckline shape, it is sometimes preferable to interface the entire neckline and yoke section as shown in the illustrations for the square and V-necklines.

Cut the interfacing on the same grain as the garment section. Trim $\frac{1}{2}$ inch from all seam allowances, and **steam-press to fuse** the interfacing to the garment section as instructed on page 16.

To cover the interfacing and finish the neckline edge, use either of the following methods, depending on the size of the section.

1. For a small section, such as the square neckline [F], cut the facing the same size as the section. Finish it the same way as a regular neckline facing.

2. So that a large section, such as the V-neckline [G], will not be too bulky, cut a soft fabric underlining for the garment section. Treat the interfaced garment section and the underlining as one layer of fabric. Cut a neckline facing of standard width from the fashion fabric, and stitch it to the interfaced garment section and underlining. Press; then trim, turn, and understitch the neckline. Hand-tack the free edge of the facing to the underlining.

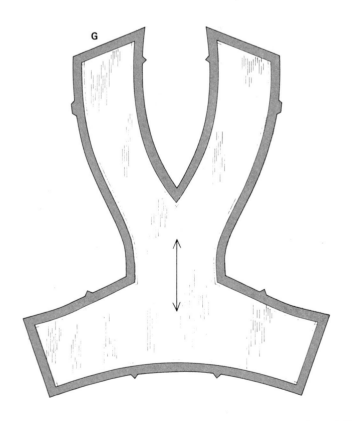

Interfaced Neckline Facing

When using a soft fabric, make a test with a scrap to make sure that the edge of the fused interfacing does not show as a line on the right side of the fabric. If a line does show, plan to fuse the interfacing to the facing instead of to the garment fabric.

For all necklines except a V-neckline, cut the interfacing by the facing pattern on the pattern grain line. **For a V-neckline,** cut the interfacing so that the lengthwise grain is parallel to the neckline edge. Trim $\frac{1}{2}$ inch from all seam allowances, and trim $\frac{1}{4}$ inch from the unnotched edge. Fuse the interfacing to the facing. Stitch the facing seams at the shoulder and at the center front. Press the seam allowances open; then trim them to one-half width as shown in illustration [A].

To finish the facing, stitch $\frac{3}{8}$ inch from the unnotched edge through the facing and interfacing [B]. Pink edges of fabrics that ravel; leave the edges straight-cut on fabrics that do not ravel. The facing is now ready to be applied to the neckline.

Shaped Band

A shaped band that may be used as a neckline finish instead of a facing is similar to a facing, except that it is turned to the outside of the garment, and the edge opposite the neckline is topstitched to the garment to form the band [C].

Fuse the interfacing to the band instead of to the garment to make the band smooth and firm. Finish the edge of the band with self-lining, or, if the fashion fabric is bulky, use a thin, crisp lining fabric of a matching color.

Cut the fusible interfacing by the band pattern section. Trim the entire $\frac{5}{8}$ inch seam allowance from the outer edges and from the center back of the interfacing. If you are making a decorative band similar to the one in the illustration, trim the points diagonally $\frac{1}{4}$ inch inside the seam lines to reduce bulk when the points are turned [D]. Trim $\frac{1}{2}$ inch from the neckline and shoulder seam allowances of the interfacing. *Steam-press to fuse.*

After fusing the interfacing to the band section, assemble the band sections at the shoulders, and assemble the band lining also. Press the shoulder seam allowances open, and trim to one-half width.

With right sides together, pin together the assembled band and lining, and stitch the outer edges on the seam line. *Do not stitch through the interfacing* [E]. Trim the seam allowances to uneven widths, $\frac{1}{4}$ inch for the band, $\frac{1}{8}$ inch for the lining. Notch curved seam allowances $\frac{1}{2}$ inch apart, and slash inside corners almost to the stitching. Press as stitched; then press seam allowances open. Turn the band right side out, turning sharply on the stitching. Hand-baste the turned edges to favor the outside. Press; then baste the lining and band together at the neckline.

Prepare the garment unit next. With the wrong

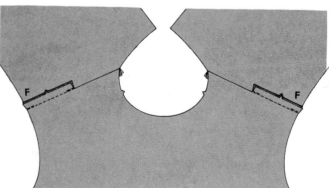

sides of the fabric together so that the seam will be on the right side of the garment, stitch the portion of the shoulder seams that will be under the band. Slash through the seam allowances to the stitching. With the right sides of the garment together, stitch the remainder of each shoulder seam [F]. Press the seam allowances open. Trim the seam allowances that will be under the band to one-half width.

To attach the band and finish the neckline and center back, turn the garment wrong side out. Pin the band to the neckline with the right side of the band to the wrong side of the garment. Stitch around the neckline, and stitch the center back only as far as the bottom of the band. Slash through the back seam allowances at the bottom of the band. Trim the back and neckline seam allowances to uneven widths. Slash the neckline seam allowances the same as for a facing. Press, and turn the band to the outside. Baste the neckline edge to favor the outside; press. Baste the outer edge to the garment, and topstitch the band and neckline $\frac{1}{4}$ or $\frac{3}{8}$ inch from the edges. Refer to the fashion drawing [C] on opposite page.

Standing Neckband

A round neckline may be finished either with a one-piece or a two-piece standing band. Make the band double, and interface both layers with lightweight, fusible interfacing to provide firmness.

For a one-piece band, cut two pieces of fusible interfacing by the band pattern. With a tracing wheel and tracing paper, mark seam lines and shoulder dots on one layer of interfacing. Cut off $\frac{1}{2}$ inch from all interfacing seam allowances, allowing $\frac{1}{8}$ inch to extend into seam allowances. *Steam-press to fuse* interfacing to wrong sides of both band layers. Pin and stitch the bands together on seam lines, taking two stitches across the inside corner at the center front, and taking one stitch across the right-angle corners at the back. Cut seam allowances to uneven widths, $\frac{1}{4}$ inch for the outside layer and $\frac{1}{8}$ inch for the inside or facing layer. Cut both corners diagonally, $\frac{1}{16}$ inch from the stitching on both layers.

At the center front, slash diagonally into each corner almost to the stitching line [G]. Finger-press seam allowances open, and turn band right side out. Transfer shoulder markings to the outside layers, using tailor's tacks through both layers. Stitching through all of the layers at the same time, stitch the band to the neckline on the seam lines. Press all seam allowances downward. On fabrics that require a seam finish, stitch the seam edges together. A neckline facing is not required for a one-piece band.

For a two-piece band, interface the neckline of the garment, and apply the band between the garment and the facing.

Interface, stitch, and turn the right and left hand sections of the band the same way as for a one-piece neckband. Hand-tack the finished pieces together on the seam line at the center front [H].

Prepare the garment with fusible interfacing the same way as for a faced round neckline. Refer to page 16.

Pin, baste, and stitch the neckband and facing to the neckline, placing right side of the neckband to right side of the garment and the right side of the facing to wrong side of the neckband. Trim seam allowances to uneven widths. Clip into seam allowances along the curves, and understitch through the facing and all seam allowances. Spot-fuse the facing at shoulder seams, at center front, and at the center-back opening. Refer to *Holding Facings in Place* on page 23.

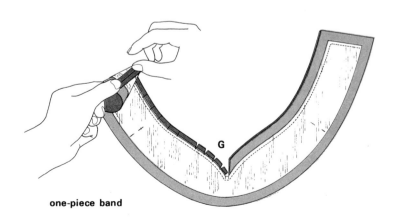

one-piece band

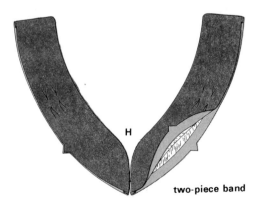

two-piece band

Collarless Neckline,
Vest Front, and Armholes

Although a fashion vest does not always have an interfacing, most styles do look better with interfacing. Vests without interfacing are made either of firm fabric that does not need interfacing or of a soft, supple fabric that gives a flowing look to the vest. There are several ways to use fusible interfacing in a vest.

A one-piece interfacing will give maximum shaping to the shoulders. Cut the neckline and armhole fusible interfacings in one piece as in [A] below. Extend the interfacing $\frac{1}{8}$ inch into the seam allowances. ***Steam-press to fuse*** the interfacing to the wrong side of the fashion fabric.

A two-piece interfacing is best for medium-weight fabrics. Use lightweight fusible interfacing and cut separate neckline and armhole interfacings as in [B] below. Always cut fusible interfacing for an armhole so that a seam is at the shoulder. Make patterns for the armhole interfacing sections by tracing the back and front vest pattern pieces. Extend the interfacing $\frac{1}{8}$ inch into all seam allowances. ***Steam-press to fuse*** the interfacing to the wrong side of the fashion fabric.

For an unlined vest with a two-piece facing, cut the front and back facings the same shape as the two-piece interfacing, but $\frac{5}{8}$ inch wider so that the facing will cover the interfacing entirely. (*This construction is not illustrated.*)

Join the armhole facing sections together into a unit; then, join the garment sections together into a separate unit.

To assemble the facing and garment sections, first, stitch and trim the seam allowances; then, turn the facing to the inside of the vest. Baste the turned edges, and press.

To hold the stitched facing edges in place, topstitch the neckline, fronts, and armholes; or understitch along the back neckline and armholes to keep the facings from rolling to the outside.

To hold the vest and facing seam allowances together, baste a $\frac{3}{4}$-inch-wide strip of fusible webbing over the facing shoulder seam allowances, and to hold the facing edges to the vest, baste a $\frac{1}{2}$-inch-wide strip

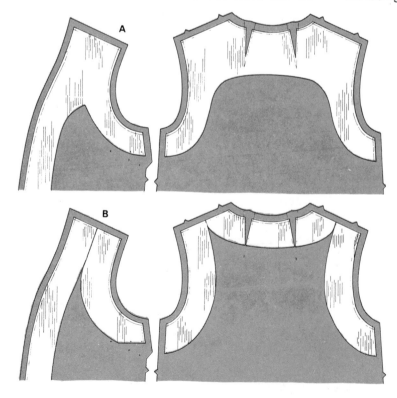

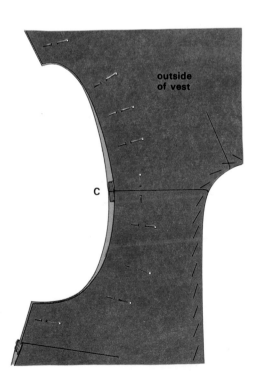

outside of vest

of fusible webbing to the interfacing, near the edge. *Steam-press to fuse.*

For an unlined vest with a one-piece facing, follow the procedure below for a fully lined vest.

For a fully lined vest with its lining extending to the neckline and armhole edges, either a one-piece or a two-piece interfacing is appropriate. Cut the vest and lining by the same pattern. Fuse the interfacing to the vest sections.

For convenience, always stitch, trim, and turn the neckline and front edges before stitching the underarm seams so that you can work on the vest while it is opened flat. Complete all steps for the neckline and front facings. Make certain that the front edges are basted with the seam slightly to the underside so that the seam favors the right side; then do the final pressing. See illustration [C] on page 20.

With the vest turned right side out, pin the lining smoothly underneath the garment fabric along the shoulder seam and between the neckline and armholes. Notice that the lining extends beyond the garment fabric near the top of the armholes [C] because the seams at the neckline and front edges were turned to favor the outside layer. The amount of excess lining would be doubled later if the *armhole* seams were again turned to favor the outside layer. An adjustment of the lining at the armhole edge should be made at this stage of construction.

Make this adjustment by cutting off *double* the amount of lining that extends beyond the garment fabric at the armhole [D], tapering from nothing at the back of the underarm, to the greatest width at the shoulder line, and tapering again to nothing at the front of the underarm.

Turn the garment and lining right sides together, and bring the cut armhole edges of the garment and lining together. Stitch the armhole seams, stopping 1 inch from underarm seam lines [E]. Trim seam allowances to uneven widths [F], and clip every ½ inch along the back and front armhole curves. After pressing the seam allowances open, turn the vest right side out by drawing each front to the back between the shoulder seams of the lining and vest.

Stitch the underarm seams of both the lining and vest. Press the seam allowances open; then stitch the small opening in the armhole seam across the underarm seam [G]. Baste around the armhole edges, placing the seam to favor the right side; then press. The lining will fit smoothly, and will not show along the edges of the armholes.

For an unlined vest without topstitching, lightweight, fusible interfacing can be applied so that it can be *fused to the facing* after the edges have been stitched and turned. This method has two important advantages. It is unnecessary to use topstitching and understitching to hold the facing under at the seam edge. Fusible interfacing can be used with fabrics that otherwise would show an impression of the interfacing. This method requires careful workmanship, and it is not for a casual sewer. (Illustrated on page 22.)

Both the armhole facing and interfacing must have a seam at the shoulder and underarm. Cut lightweight, fusible interfacing by the facing pattern. *Do not* cut off the interfacing seam allowances, but *do* cut off ½ inch from the unnotched edges.

Stitch darts in the front and back vest, and press. Pin the *unfusible* side of the interfacing against the *wrong side* of the back and front vest sections. Stay-

underside of vest

D

F

E

G

stitch through the interfacing and garment a scant ⅝ inch from the seam edges [H].

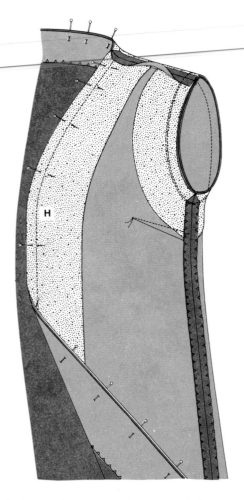

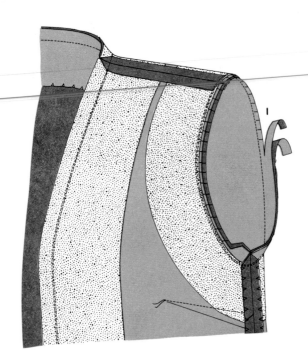

Note: *Further on in construction, the interfacing will be fused to the facing, and the trimmed seam allowances will then be held captive between the interfacing and the facing.*

Stitch the shoulder seams, and trim interfacing seam allowances outside of the stitching. Using a seam board, press the shoulder seam allowances open. *Do not let the iron touch the interfacing!*

Stitch the back and front neckline facings together at the shoulders. Stitch the armhole facing sections together at the shoulders and underarms. Press all facing seam allowances open, and trim to one-half width. Finish the unnotched facing edges and under-arm seam allowances with edge stitching, binding, or machine overcasting.

Pin the neckline and armhole facings to the vest, right sides together. The facings must fit the garment exactly; if they do not, it is usually because the seam allowances have not been stitched to the same width. *Correct the fit now; it cannot be done later!*

Stitch the facings to the neckline, front, and arm-holes just inside the stay stitching. Trim interfacing seam allowances just outside the stay stitching. Trim *vest* seam allowances to ⅛ inch and *facing* seam allowances to ¼ inch; this is the reverse of the way it is

usually done. Slash seam allowances on inside curves [I], and notch seam allowances on outside curves so that they will flatten when they are turned to the inside. Finger-press seam allowances open. Turn facings to the inside, and hand-baste near the turned edge. Smooth the facing against the interfacing with your fingertips, and baste the loose edges of the facing and interfacing to the vest. As you baste near the shoulder and underarm seams, slip strips of ¾-inch-wide fusible webbing between the garment and the facing seam allowances, and catch the webbing in the basting stitches.

From the facing side, **steam-press to fuse,** pressing with each application of the iron only as much as will flatten over a press mitt or a sleeve board [J], and press only as far as 6 inches from the bottom of the vest. While the garment is still warm, clip and remove the basting thread piece by piece. With the vest right side up, cover the fabric with a thin press cloth, and press it again only as far as the unfused 6 inches at the bottom of the vest. Refer to page 60 for inter-facing the hem.

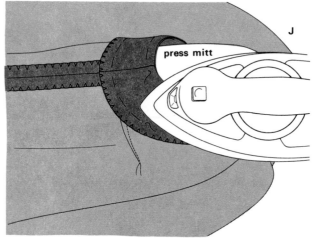

press mitt

ARMHOLE INTERFACINGS

Sleeveless armholes should be both faced and interfaced. Fusible interfacing is ideal for this purpose because it will move as one with the garment fabric, will not curl, and will provide an inside layer to which the facing edges can be fastened. Fasten the facing edges by using small, appropriately shaped pieces of fusible webbing to fuse the facing to the interfacing as described in *Armhole Facing,* below.

Cut the fusible interfacing for the armhole by the front and back pattern sections. Cut off ½ inch from the edge that does not have a seam allowance, and let the interfacing extend ⅛ inch into all seam allowances. *Steam-press to fuse* the interfacing to the wrong side of the fashion fabric.

HOLDING FACINGS IN PLACE

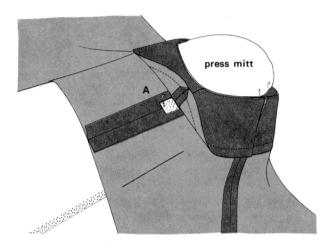

To hold a facing in place so that it is almost invisible, fuse a narrow strip of fusible webbing between the seam allowances of the garment and the facing. Fuse webbing between the interfacing and facing at places where there could be strain.

Neckline Facing

For a round neckline, cut a ⅝-inch-wide strip of fusible webbing as long as the measurement from the understitching to the facing edge. Place the webbing between the shoulder seam allowances of the garment and the facing [A]. With the facing side up over a press mitt or a sleeve board, *steam-press to fuse.*

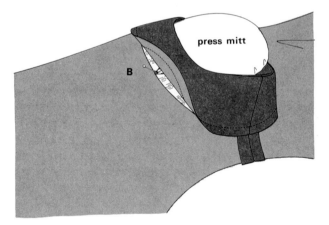

At the center front, insert a triangle of fusible webbing between the facing and the interfacing. Make the triangle about 1 inch wide at the neckline, and taper it to a point at the edge of the facing [B]. *Steam-press to fuse.*

At the zipper closure, turn under the facing edge, and press a crease. Insert a ⅜-inch-wide strip of webbing between the folded edge of the facing and the zipper tape. Extend the webbing from the understitching to the edge of the facing [C]. With the zipper closed and covered with a damp press cloth for protection, *steam-press to fuse.*

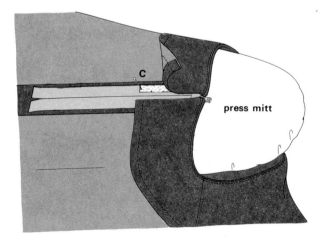

Armhole Facing

For an armhole facing, follow the same steps as for a round neckline facing. Fuse seam allowances of the garment and facing together. Fuse a triangle of webbing between the facing and interfacing at the back and at the front armhole notch positions. Fuse the facing to the interfacing in just enough locations to hold the fabric in place when the garment is being worn. *Avoid overdoing it!* Too much fusing will create excessive rigidity in the garment.

ZIPPER APPLICATIONS

Depending on the compatibility of the fabric, fusible webbing and fusible interfacing can be used in a variety of ways for applying a regular zipper having a nylon or polyester coil, or metal teeth. *Invisible zippers cannot be used in fused applications.*

Fusible webbing may be used *instead of stitching* in a zipper application; fusible interfacing is used mainly to *improve the appearance* of a zipper application in a fly-front closure or where the rigidity of the zipper conflicts with the suppleness of the fashion fabric. Remember to shrink the zipper tape before applying the zipper.

Knitted and woven fabrics of medium-weight wool, polyester, or acrylic fibers are typical fabrics with which fusible materials can be used successfully. Fabrics made of other fibers or blends of fibers can be used also, but it is always advisable to test a sample of the fabric first before using fusible materials on a garment. If you have doubts about the strength of a fused zipper application, you can always add hand or machine stitching as the final step in a centered or lapped seam application. Remember that fusible webbing will not hold securely unless it has disappeared completely into the fabric after fusing.

Centered in a Seam

Use a centered zipper application for a dress, robe, jumper, or overblouse that has a center-front or center-back neckline opening, or for a fitted sleeve.

Apply the zipper before the garment sections have been assembled.

Fuse the neckline interfacing to the wrong side of the garment, letting the interfacing extend $\frac{1}{8}$ inch into the neckline and shoulder seam allowances, but only as far as the center seam line, as illustrated below.

Determine how long the basted portion of the seam should be by measuring it with a zipper that has been shrunk. Cut the tape $\frac{1}{2}$ inch above the top stop. Place the zipper on the seam allowance with the cut end of the tape against the neckline seam line. At the bottom stop, place a pin across the seam line to mark the bottom end of the basted seam [A].

With a 12-stitch length, stitch the seam from the bottom up to the pin that marks the bottom of the basted seam; then backstitch. Cut both the needle thread and the bobbin thread; then with a 6-stitch length, machine-baste the placket opening. Now cut only the needle thread at the top, near the neckline edge. Let the bobbin thread extend for 3 or 4 inches so that when you are ready to pull out the basting, you can grasp the thread firmly [B]. At about 1-inch intervals, cut the needle thread in the basting for easy removal further on.

Press the entire seam twice; first to embed the stitches, then to press the seam allowances open.

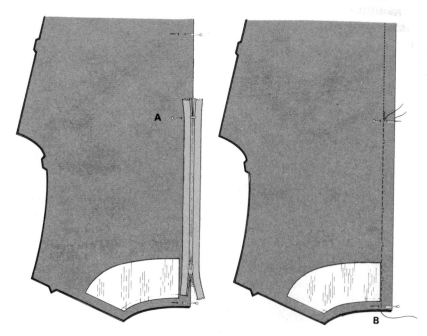

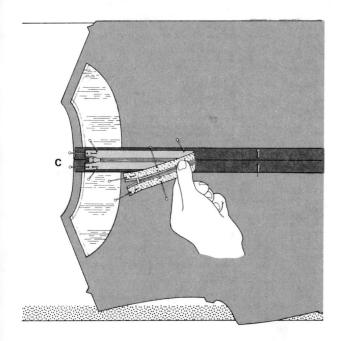

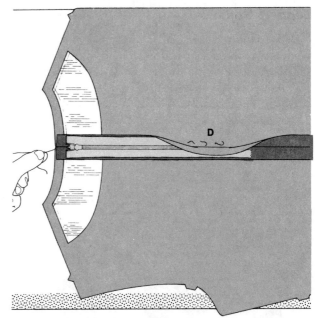

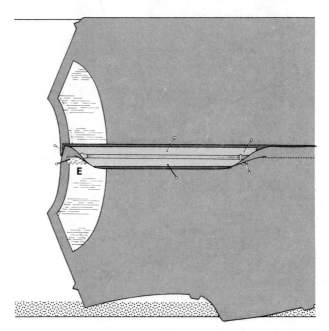

To prepare the zipper, pin a ³⁄₈-inch-wide strip of fusible webbing to the right side of each zipper tape. Align the webbing so that it extends precisely from the edge of the tape to the cord alongside the edge of the zipper coil. Except at the ends, place pins 4 or 5 inches apart perpendicular to the tape. At the ends, place the pins parallel to the tape. It is convenient to use ³⁄₄-inch-wide fusible webbing for this application because the straight-cut strips need to be cut only through the center.

Working on the ironing board, with the zipper pull-tab up and the zipper right side down, position the zipper with the cut ends of the tapes against the neckline. Pin the ends in place. To make it easy to center the coil on the seam, roll back the zipper and pin the edges of the tape to the seam allowances 4 or 5 inches apart, plunging the pins through the garment and into the padding of the ironing board at an angle [C]. Cover the zipper with a damp press cloth, and **steam-press to fuse.**

Remove the basting; first, by pulling out the long bobbin thread at the neckline; then, by turning up the seam allowance and removing the cut basting threads from the other side [D].

To complete the application, use *pinking shears* to cut lengthwise through the center of ³⁄₄-inch-wide fusible webbing to make two ³⁄₈-inch-wide strips that are ¹⁄₂ inch longer than the zipper coil. With the garment wrong side up on the ironing board, pin a strip of webbing under each seam allowance with the pinked edge toward the edge of the seam allowance [E], and **steam-press to fuse.** Turn the garment section right side up, and again, **steam-press to fuse.** The steam-pressing on the right side should ensure complete fusing for maximum strength [F].

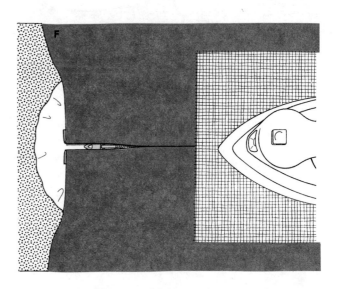

Lapped Seam

Use a lapped seam zipper application in the side seam of a skirt, pants, or dress, or in the center-front or center-back seam of a dress, blouse, or jumper.

In a side seam, apply the zipper after the garment has been partially assembled and carefully fitted.

In a center seam, apply the zipper before the garment sections have been assembled.

Fuse the neckline interfacing to the wrong side of the garment, letting the interfacing extend $\frac{1}{8}$ inch into the neckline and shoulder seam allowances, but only as far as the center seam line.

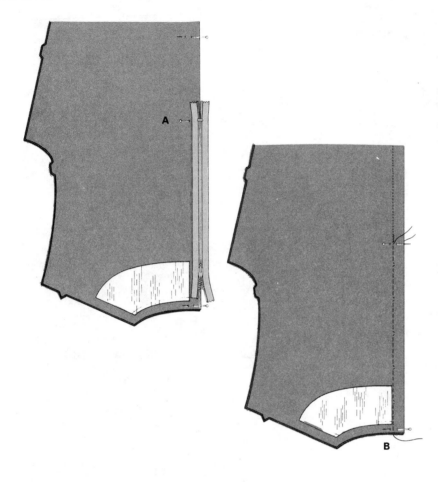

Determine how long the basted portion of the seam should be by measuring it with a zipper that has been shrunk. Cut the tape $\frac{1}{2}$ inch above the top stop. Place the zipper on the seam allowance with the cut end of the tape against the neckline seam line. At the bottom stop, place a pin across the seam line to mark the bottom end of the basted seam [A].

With a 12-stitch length, stitch the seam from the bottom up to the pin that marks the bottom of the basted seam; then backstitch. Cut both the needle thread and the bobbin thread; then with a 6-stitch length, machine-baste the placket opening. Now cut only the needle thread at the top, near the neckline edge. Let the bobbin thread extend for 3 or 4 inches so that when you are ready to remove the basting, you can grasp the thread firmly. At about 1-inch intervals, cut the needle thread in the basting for easy removal further on [B].

Press the entire seam to embed the stitches. Press open both seam allowances of the *permanently stitched* part of the seam only. Press open only the *one* seam allowance of the basted seam that *will lap over the zipper;* let the other side remain extended [C].

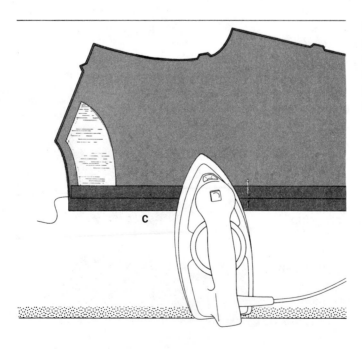

Place the open zipper face down on the extended seam allowance with the top stop $\frac{1}{2}$ inch below the neckline seam line and with the bottom stop at the bottom of the basting. Hold the zipper coil on the seam line. With the zipper foot to the right of the needle, machine-baste from the bottom upward along the tape guidelines [D].

Close the zipper and turn it face up. Using a 12-stitch length and with the zipper foot to the left of the needle, topstitch from the bottom upward, stitching through the folded seam allowance and the zipper tape [E].

Shift the position of the garment so that the other seam allowance is extended, and turn the zipper face down over it. Cut a $\frac{3}{4}$-inch-wide strip of fusible webbing as long as the basted seam, and place it under the extended seam allowance. If the seam is shaped—as a side seam, for example—shape the strip of webbing to conform. Position one edge of the webbing along the basted seam line; the other edge will extend beyond the edge of the zipper tape. With the zipper foot to the left of the needle, stitch through the webbing, seam allowance, and zipper tape from the bottom to the top. At the top, guide the stitching closer to the seam edge to allow room for the zipper slide and pull-tab [F].

Remove the basting, gently lifting out the short threads from one side and pulling out the long threads from the other side [G]. Trim the $\frac{1}{4}$ inch of webbing that extends beyond the zipper tape.

Place the garment right side up over a press mitt. First, *steam-press to fuse* the side of the seam that overlaps, almost to the top of the placket. Then, open the zipper and *steam-press to fuse* the top portion of the placket [H].

Hand or machine topstitching may be added either for strength or appearance. The fusing step then would serve only to hold the fabric layers in place while they were being stitched.

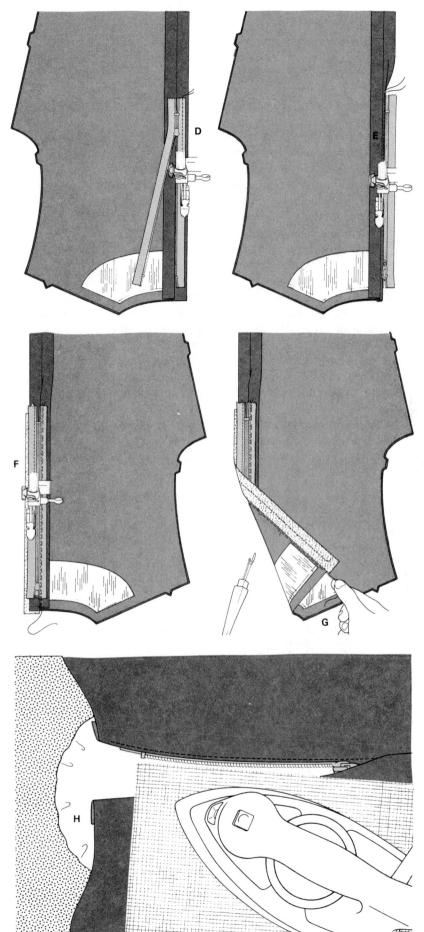

Fly-front Closure

A fly-front closure is frequently used as a design feature in expensive ready-made pants and skirts. It is a feature that would appeal to those women who are willing to devote a little more time and effort to their sewing when high-quality clothing is their goal. Patterns for skirts or pants that do not include a fly-front closure in their design can be adapted easily.

Measure and mark the pattern $7/8$ inch to the left and to the right of the center-front seam line at the waistline and at the pattern symbol that indicates the bottom of the placket. Using a ruler, draw lines that are parallel to the center-front seam line from the markings at the waistline, down to the markings at the bottom of the placket. Make sure that the lines are parallel. On the garment side, round the line at the bottom so that it intersects the center-front seam line. On the seam allowance side, round the line at the bottom identically, and add a $5/8$-inch seam allowance to the outside edge [A]. After making these changes on the pattern front section, trace them on another piece of paper. The tracing [B] is your pattern for cutting a section of lightweight, fusible interfacing. Save the tracing for use in the future to adapt other patterns.

In girls' and women's clothing the overlap may be either traditional (right over left) or mannish (left over right). Cut both front sections the same, but be sure to cut the fusible interfacing in the right direction so that the fusible side will be in contact with the garment fabric.

Fuse the interfacing to the wrong side of the right front. Using even basting that can be seen on the wrong side as well as on the right side, mark the left and right center-front seam lines [C] between the tailor's tacks that indicate the top and bottom of the placket opening. Using short, even basting, baste alongside the edge of the interfacing [D]. This basting is the guideline for topstitching the placket.

For a skirt, stitch the center-front seam from the bottom of the skirt to the bottom of the placket, backstitching at both ends of the stitching.

For pants, start at the tailor's tacks at the bottom of the placket, and stitch the front sections together, stopping 1 inch from the inside-leg seam lines; backstitch at both ends of the stitching.

Select a skirt or neckline zipper that is longer than the placket opening. The extra length at the top will be cut off further on in construction, and the waistband stitching will become the top stop. Shrink, dry, and lightly press the zipper tape before applying it.

Position the zipper *right side down* on the underside of the fly closure, but on the *right* side of the fabric. Place the edge of the zipper tape along the center-front basting line with the bottom stop $3/4$ inch from the seam edge. With the zipper foot to the left of the needle, stitch from the bottom upward along the edge of the tape. Then, with the zipper foot to the right of the needle, stitch near the zipper coil [E].

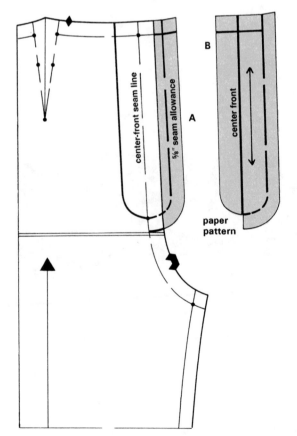

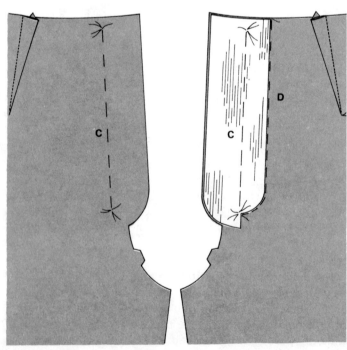

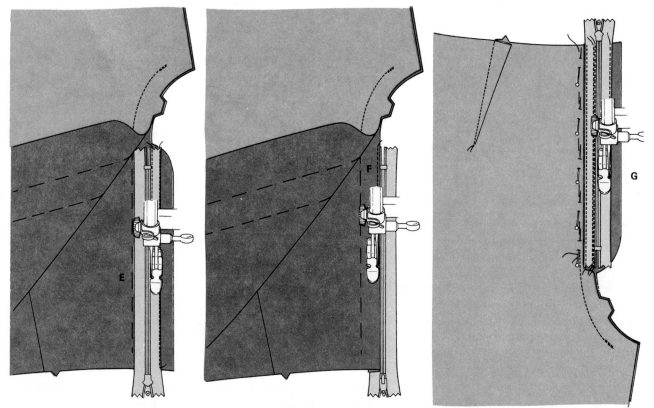

Turn the zipper right side up on this stitching line, and topstitch the fold [F]. Trim any fabric that extends beyond the zipper tape.

Next, prepare to stitch the unattached edge of the zipper tape to the fly. Pin or baste together the right and left center-front basting lines from the bottom of the placket opening to the waistline seam edge. Be careful; place one line of basting over the other exactly. With the zipper foot to the left of the needle [G], stitch along the edge of the zipper tape from top to bottom.

This stitching safeguards against slight inaccuracies in measuring. Although the final stitching should catch the zipper tape evenly near the edge, it sometimes misses for short distances. With this hidden stitching, the zipper will be fastened securely and not be wholly dependent on the topstitching.

Remove the pins or basting from the center front, and turn the garment right side up. Protect the fabric with a thin press cloth, and press lightly along the center-front fold of the overlap. *Do not press over the zipper!*

With the zipper foot to the left of the needle, stitch the garment from the top downward at the right of the basting [H]. Backstitch one stitch where the topstitching intersects the front fold. Draw the threads to the underside and tie.

Remove the basting and press the closure over a press mitt, using a thin press cloth to protect the right side of the garment. Do not cut the surplus length from the zipper at the waistline; wait until the waistband is stitched across the opened placket. The waistband stitching will serve as the stop.

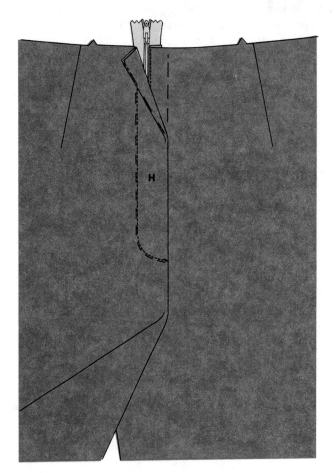

IN-THE-SEAM BUTTONHOLES

Many patterns can be converted from bound or machine buttonholes to vertical in-the-seam buttonholes, which impart a distinctive look of quality to a fashion garment.

If the garment will always be worn closed or buttoned, change the right front only; if it will be worn open or unbuttoned, change the right and the left fronts. Back closings on women's clothing lap right over left, the same as in front closures.

1. Cut off one side (or both sides) of the garment $\frac{1}{2}$ inch outside the center line, or the buttonhole position line if the buttonholes are not centered. Do the same to the facing. Cut a straight-grain strip of fabric *twice* as wide as the pattern measures from the center line to finished edge *plus 1 inch* for two $\frac{1}{2}$-inch seam allowances.

Mark the garment and the facing edges by clipping $\frac{1}{4}$ inch into the seam allowances at the top and bottom of each buttonhole [A]. Be sure these markings are in corresponding positions. Pin one side of the straight-grain strip to the garment edge, the other side to the facing edge. At each clip, place pins perpendicular to the seam line to indicate the buttonhole ends [B].

Taking $\frac{1}{2}$-inch seam allowances, stitch from the neckline above the first buttonhole, between all buttonholes, to below the bottom buttonhole. Backstitch at the neckline and at the top and bottom of each buttonhole, but *do not cut* the needle and bobbin threads. Carry the threads over each buttonhole opening intact. This method prevents raveling, and eliminates tying the thread ends. Press the stitching; then press the seam allowances open.

2. Select lightweight, fusible interfacing, and cut it so that each section extends $\frac{1}{8}$ inch into the neckline seam allowance and just to the seam lines of the center strip and of the garment front, $\frac{1}{2}$ inch from the inside edge of the facing. ***Steam-press to fuse*** the interfacing both to the garment and to the center strip.

Cut $\frac{1}{4}$-inch-wide strips of fusible webbing, and place

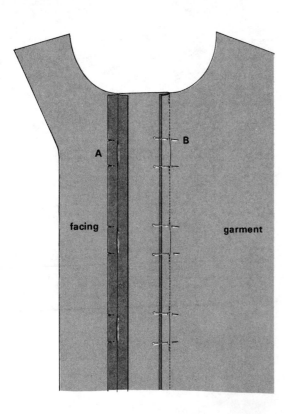

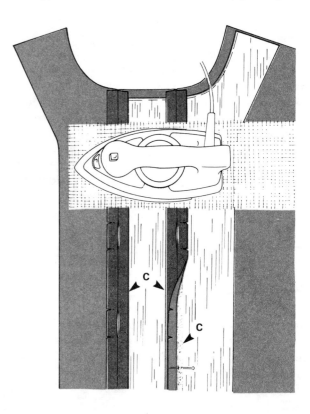

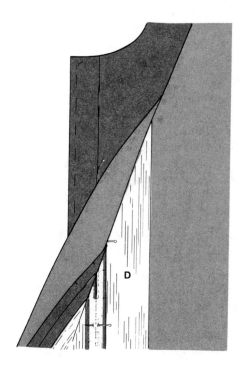

them under the seam allowance ot the garment and under the two seam allowances of the center strip [C]. ***Steam-press to fuse*** the seam allowances to the interfacing. If the fashion fabric will not hold a sharply pressed crease, place a $\frac{1}{4}$-inch-wide strip of webbing under the facing seam allowance, then ***steam-press to fuse.***

3. Fold the center strip, matching the seam allowances and the openings for the buttonholes. Press to form the edge crease. Before finishing the buttonholes, finish the neckline and hem. Then, refold on the edge crease, and hand-baste $\frac{1}{2}$ inch inside the edge crease to hold the layers securely.

4. To finish the buttonholes, prepare a $\frac{3}{4}$- to 1-inch-wide strip of fusible webbing as long as the measurement from the neckline to the top of the hem. Cut $\frac{1}{8}$-inch-wide windows in the center of the webbing so that they match the buttonhole openings exactly [D].

Working on the ironing board, pin the prepared webbing over the garment seam allowances, and cover the webbing with the facing seam allowances. Transfer the pins from the inside of the garment to the outside of the facing as you work. First, from the facing side of the garment, ***steam-press to fuse.*** Then, from the right side of the garment, ***steam-press to fuse.***

PATCH POCKETS AND POCKET FLAPS

Patch pockets are often shown in pattern guides with seam allowances turned under and with the pockets topstitched to the garment. Although this simple procedure may be effective on a few easy-to-sew fabrics, for most fabrics, one or two additional elements such as fusible interfacing and lining will improve patch pockets considerably. The interfacing adds body, making the pocket more prominent; the lining gives a smoothly rounded edge, making the pocket look neater.

Lined Patch Pocket

Curved edges can be finished faster and better with a lining than by simply turning under the seam allowance and using topstitching. Cut a lining of self-fabric or of a thinner fabric as long and as wide as the pocket.

Always use a straight-stitch presser foot to stitch a curved seam because it is easier to guide the stitching accurately. Except for the top edge, cut off the pocket seam allowances to ¼ inch to make guiding the stitching even easier.

To join the top edge of the pocket facing to the top edge of the lining, take a full ⅝-inch seam; use permanent stitching for about 1 inch at each end, and backstitch. Use machine basting across the center. The basting will be removed later to permit the pocket to be turned right side out. Press both seam allowances downward, and with right sides together, lightly crease the pocket facing on the pattern markings. Pin the pocket and lining as shown [A] to keep the layers from shifting.

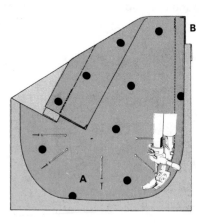

Using the straight-stitch presser foot and with the trimmed pocket up, stitch and backstitch ¼ inch from the cut edge [B]. Backstitch at one corner, and continue to stitch around the pocket to the opposite corner, ending with backstitching. Trim the seam allowances of the pocket facing and lining to ⅛ inch [C]. On

firm fabrics, cut wedges from the fabric of the seam allowance at the curves. Remove the machine basting; then finger-press the seam allowances open.

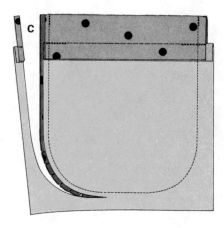

Turn the pocket right side out through the open seam [D] and again, finger-press the outside edges to make the lining turn on the stitching.

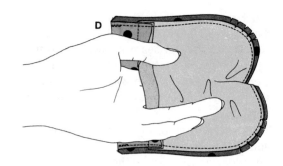

Steam-press the pocket. Insert a ¼-inch-wide strip of fusible webbing between the hem seam allowances of the pocket facing and the lining; *steam-press to fuse* [E].

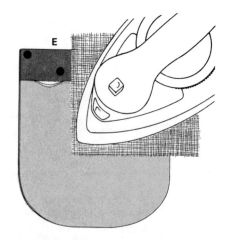

To apply the pocket, pin and baste it to the garment, matching the pattern markings, and then topstitch.

Lined Patch Pocket with Flap

Pockets on soft, medium-weight knit or woven fabrics are usually improved by applying a lightweight, fusible interfacing to the pocket and the flap. The body of the pocket may be lined either with self-fabric or a thin fabric in a matching color. Patch pockets must be made carefully; they must be *identical* in shape, and the fabric must be cut on the *straight grain*. It is best to delay cutting the pocket until after the garment sections have been cut. Then, cut the pieces reserved for the pockets into grain-perfect rectangles the approximate length and width of the pocket pattern. Lightly fuse lightweight interfacing to the rectangles. Cut the pockets, and mark the seam lines on the interfacing with tracing paper. Cut the seam allowances to $\frac{1}{4}$ inch

along the flap to $\frac{1}{8}$ inch. Trim the pocket lining seam allowance to $\frac{1}{8}$ inch. Notch the curved portions of the flap and pocket seam allowances [D]. On *both* sides of the pocket, **steam-press to fuse** to obtain maximum fusing of the interfacing. Remove the basting from the lining seam line.

Finger-press the seam allowances open, and turn the pocket right side out through the opening in the lining seam. Shape the edges with your fingertips. If necessary, baste the edges of the pockets to keep the fold on the seam line. To shape the edges, first press gently; then, firmly press the entire pocket and flap. The pocket is now ready to apply, either with hand stitching or with machine topstitching [E].

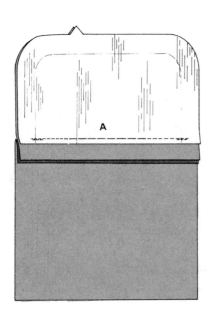

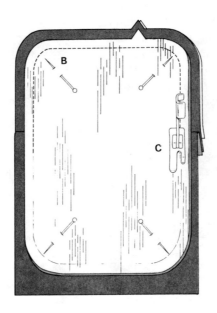

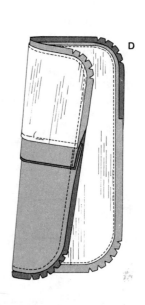

to make it easier to guide the stitching. Cut all the pocket sections before taking the next step. Compare the pocket sections for size and shape, and trim, if necessary, to make them identical. Cut flaps from interfaced fabric; then cut the lining fabric.

Pin and stitch the lining to the edge of the pocket flap, leaving the center portion machine-basted [A]. Press both seam allowances toward the bottom of the pocket, and trim the interfacing seam allowance $\frac{1}{16}$ inch outside the stitching. With right sides together, center the interfaced pocket on the lining and flap unit $\frac{3}{8}$ inch from the top and side edges. Pin at the four corners as shown [B].

Using the straight-stitch presser foot, stitch the pocket together $\frac{1}{4}$ inch from the pocket edge [C]. Press the stitching, and while the interfacing is still warm, gently separate it from the pocket seam allowance with your fingertips. Trim the interfacing $\frac{1}{16}$ inch outside the stitching. Do the same on the seam allowances around the pocket flap. Trim the flap seam allowance to $\frac{1}{4}$ inch and the pocket seam allowance

Separate Pocket Flaps

A separate pocket flap may be made by following the same procedure described for the lined pocket with flap. Lightweight, fusible interfacing may be applied to both layers of the flap, or applied only to the top layer. Make test samples from fabric scraps before you make pocket flaps for your garment.

SIMPLE BELTS

It is preferable to make a simple belt that has a centered seam because it is the same at both edges, it looks neater and smoother around the waistline, and it holds its shape better and longer than any other type of belt.

Tie Belt, Centered Seam

First, decide on the width of the finished belt. For example, assume that the finished width will be $1\frac{1}{2}$ inches. Cut the fabric on the lengthwise grain three times the finished width of the belt ($4\frac{1}{2}$ inches). Mark each seam allowance one-half the finished width ($\frac{3}{4}$ inch).

Fold the fabric strip with right sides together, and stitch $\frac{3}{4}$ inch from the edges, leaving a 2-inch-long opening at the center for turning later. Press the seam allowances open, and center the seam line. The seam allowance edges should extend to the folds exactly. Place a strip of fusible webbing under each seam allowance, and **steam-press to fuse** [A].

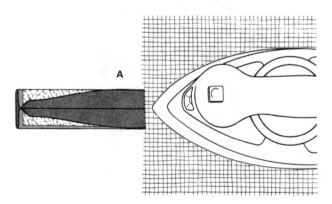

Mark a tie-point at each end. Stitch, taking two stitches across the point and backstitching at each edge. Trim seam allowances at the points [B].

Turn the belt right side out through the center opening, and work the ends smooth with your fingertips. Hand-stitch the center opening, and steam-press to finish the belt [C].

This belt can be finished with a buckle because the fused seam allowances serve as a third layer, adding sufficient strength to support a buckle.

Interfaced Belt, Centered Seam

Cut the belt fabric on the lengthwise grain twice the finished width plus two $\frac{5}{8}$-inch seam allowances. Select a fusible interfacing that has the desired rigidity for the finished belt. Cut the interfacing the same width as the finished belt.

On an ironing board, center the interfacing on the wrong side of the belt fabric, and **steam-press to fuse.** Machine-baste near the edges of the interfacing to keep the edges from rolling when you turn the belt [D]. With right sides together, fold the fabric strip in half lengthwise.

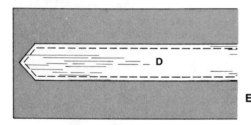

Stitch on the seam line [E], leaving a 2-inch opening at the center for turning later. Press seam allowances open, and center the seam on the belt. Trim the seam allowances to $\frac{1}{4}$ inch.

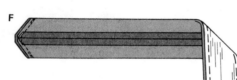

Mark a point at each end, and stitch, taking two stitches across the point and backstitching at each edge. Trim seam allowances at the points [F].

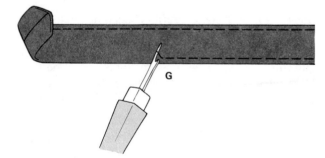

If the fabric will not crease sharply, insert strips of fusible webbing under the seam allowances, and **steam-press to fuse.** Turn the belt to the right side, and remove the machine basting [G]. Hand-stitch the center opening, then steam-press. Topstitch if desired.

WAISTBANDS

The waistbands of pants or skirts may close on the left, center front, or center back, depending on the design of the garment. Usually the ends of the waistband lap from $2\frac{1}{2}$ to $3\frac{1}{2}$ inches, but the exact width depends on personal preference, the size of the garment, or the width of the zipper underlay if one is used. The waistband may extend either beyond one of the placket edges, forming an overlap or an underlap, or it may extend beyond both placket edges.

Interfacing always improves a waistband. It adds support, firmness, loft, and in most garments, a wrinkle-free appearance. Choose the type of interfacing that will give the characteristics you want in your finished waistband. If you are not sure which one to choose, make a short test sample, using each interfacing and method that you are considering.

Soft Waistband

You can use either a nonwoven, fusible interfacing or a regular, nonwoven interfacing plus fusible webbing. Remember that there are different weights, textures, and fibers in the various brands and types of interfacings.

Cut the waistband on the lengthwise grain of the fabric twice the width of the finished waistband plus two $\frac{5}{8}$-inch seam allowances. For example, for a 1-inch-wide waistband, cut the fabric $3\frac{1}{4}$ inches wide.

For the length, measure your waistline for a comfortable fit, but not as snugly as you would measure for determining your pattern size. Add 1 inch to the waistline measurement for forming a point at the upper side of the placket plus $2\frac{1}{2}$ inches for the underlap and seam allowance on the underside of the placket. If your garment does not have an underlay attached to the zipper, extend the waistband just the same. Mark the waistband for the fabric allowances that were added at the ends; the measurement of the entire length of the waistband fabric, minus the amount added at the ends, should equal your waistline measurement. Because a garment must be eased to the waistband, the waistline of a skirt or pants should measure more than the waistband; otherwise it will look strained just below the waistline when you are wearing it.

With wrong sides together, fold the waistband fabric lengthwise through the center and press to crease, from one end to the other.

Cut nonwoven, fusible interfacing (or plain interfacing plus fusible webbing) the width of the finished waistband and as long as the waistband fabric minus the seam allowances at each end. Cut one end to a point.

Working on an ironing board, place the interfacing, fusible side down, on the wrong side of the face of the waistband with an edge alongside the crease. **Steam-press to fuse.** The interfacing acts as a shield

to prevent the seam allowance from showing as a ridge on the outside of the finished waistband.

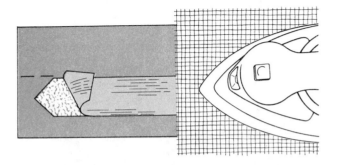

Pin and baste the waistband to the waistline of the garment, taking care to distribute the ease equally. Stitch alongside the interfacing, not through it, and backstitch at both ends of the stitching.

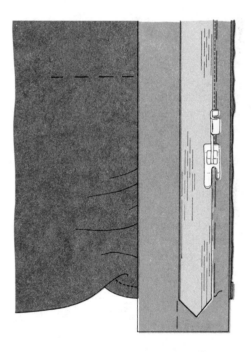

Remove the basting and press the line of stitching. Turn the waistband up, and from the right side, press the seam line of the waistband, using a press cloth to protect the fabric. Trim the waistline seam allowances to $\frac{1}{4}$ inch, and clip the darts and corners of crossing seam allowances.

Finish the free edge of the waistband with machine overedge stitching, or with straight stitching, placed $\frac{1}{4}$ inch from the edge of the seam allowance. Pink the edge of the seam allowance if the fabric is woven; leave it straight-cut if it is knitted.

At the pointed end, fold the waistband, right sides together, along the top of the interfacing. Stitch alongside the interfacing, taking one or two stitches straight across at the point. Backstitch at both ends of the stitching.

Fold the opposite end of the waistband, right sides together, along the top of the interfacing. Stitch across the end. If the closure has an underlay, as shown in the illustration below, this stitching should fall at the edge of the underlay and the end of the interfacing.

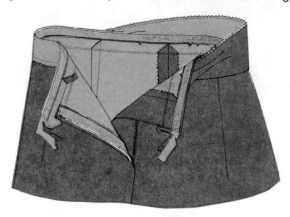

If the closure does not have an underlay, place the stitching at the end of the interfacing. Pivot and stitch, following the lower edge of the interfacing as far as the zipper tape.

Trim seam allowances to uneven widths, $\frac{1}{4}$ and $\frac{1}{8}$ inch, and trim at the corners. Turn the ends to the right side, ease out the corners, and press.

Turn the free edge of the waistband to the inside along the top edge of the interfacing. Pin the free edge to the garment, matching the seam lines. The seam-allowance edge of the unstitched side of the waistband will extend below the seam line. Turn under the seam allowance where the waistband crosses the zipper tape at the front. Hand-baste the remainder of the unstitched side to the seam line. Finish by hand with a

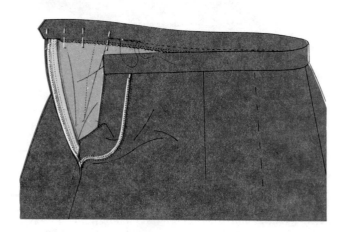

backstitch, catching only the seam allowance and waistband so that the stitches will not be visible on the outside; or machine-stitch in the crevice of the waistline seam from the outside, using the zipper foot. The machine-stitched way is best for knits, but it is optional for woven fabrics. Finish by sewing on hooks and eyes.

Firm Waistband

For a firm waistband, use fusible webbing to attach hair-canvas interfacing to the wrong side of the waistband fabric. Extend the interfacing to the seam lines of the face and ends, and $\frac{1}{2}$ inch into the seam allowance of the back of the waistband.

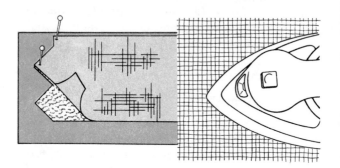

Finish the seam-allowance edge of the back of the waistband with a machine overedge stitch, or turn under the edge and edgestitch.

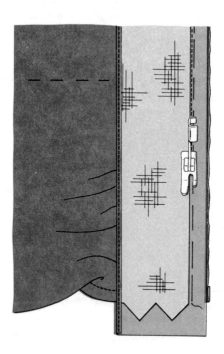

To apply the waistband to the garment, follow the procedure for a soft waistband on page 35.

HEMS

Fusible webbing eliminates the task of finishing hems in fabrics that are difficult to penetrate with a hand-sewing needle. In fabrics with a high degree of cross-wise stretch, it eliminates the annoyance caused by broken hand stitches. Loosely woven tweeds and knits of polyester and acrylic are typical examples of fabrics that are best suited for hemming with fusible webbing.

Fusible webbing can be used successfully to put up a hem only if you prepare the hem in advance as carefully as you would prepare a hand-stitched hem, and *then* apply the webbing. The following steps apply to the preparation either of a straight or a curved hem.

1. Mark the hemline with pins or chalk on the person who will wear the garment.

2. Fold the hem on the chalk or pin line, and place pins at right angles to the folded edge. The fold of the hem should follow an even line. Adjust any irregularities that might have been caused by unevenness of

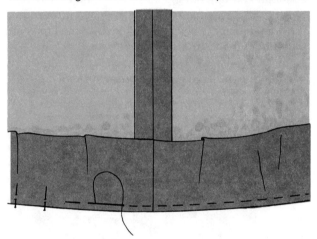

the floor, body sway, or movement. *Do not make radical adjustments.* Baste the hem ¼ inch from the folded edge. Press to sharpen the crease, moving the iron in the direction of the lengthwise grain of the fabric.

3. Even the hem width by measuring, marking, and cutting away the excess width. Then, trim all crossing

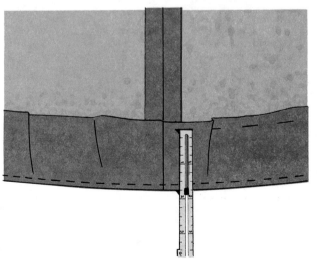

seam allowances to one-half width from the fold to the hem edge. Press again to shape the hem to the garment across the entire width of the hem.

If you are working on a straight hem, follow the instructions below; for a curved hem, see page 38.

Straight Hem

Finish the hem edge as simply as possible. On fabrics that do not fray, use straight stitching ¼ inch from a straight-cut edge. On fabrics that fray, such as woven tweed or sweater knit, use a zigzag edge-finishing stitch or a straight machine stitch. Press to smooth the hem edge. Remove the hand basting near the fold.

Cut a length of fusible webbing that is ¼ inch narrower than the hem width. Straight-cut the edge that will extend into the hem fold, and pink the edge that will be near the top of the hem. Insert the webbing between the hem and the garment, and *steam-press to fuse.*

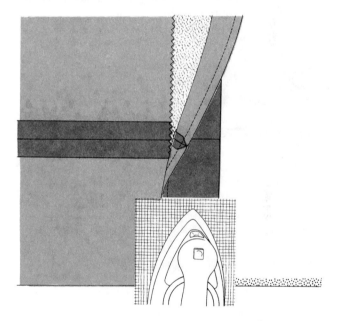

The pinked edge and the ¼-inch setback of the webbing should result in an indistinct outline instead of a sharp line along the top of the hem on the right side of the garment. If the fashion fabric is thick or tightly constructed, *steam-press to fuse* from the right side of the garment also. Remember that the fusible webbing must be changed from a solid state to a molten state by the heat and pressure applied by the iron, or it will not fuse the hem to the garment adequately. Whenever you steam-press a hem from the right side, provide additional soft padding on your ironing board to prevent the hem edge from embossing a line on the garment. A thick terry-cloth towel will serve this purpose well.

Curved or Flared Hem

Except for knife-pleated, dirndl, and gathered skirts, which have straight hems, most dress, coat, and jacket hems are curved. The top of a curved hem often measures more than the garment at the place where the hem is attached. The greater the flare and the wider the hem, the more fullness there will be to control. Before the hem is fused to the garment, the fullness in the hem must be reduced to almost nothing, otherwise bulges or wrinkles will be embossed on the outside of the garment.

After completing the three preparatory steps on page 37, stitch ¼ inch from the hem edge to make a control thread. Start and stop at each crossing seam, leaving thread ends about 3 inches long. Draw up the fullness by pulling the bobbin thread until each section conforms to the garment. Do not draw the control thread so tightly that the hem edge becomes smaller than the garment.

Steam-press the hem over a press mitt to shrink the hem fullness. On an ironing board, press the hem against the garment, moving the point of the iron from the hem fold to the hem edge. At the crossing seams, draw the control threads to the inside and tie them. If you cannot shrink the hem fullness so that the hem

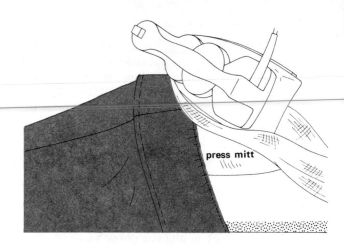

press mitt

flattens against the garment, try making the hem narrower so that it will flatten, or stitch the hem instead of fusing it.

Straight-cut the bottom edge of the fusible webbing so that it conforms to the curve of the hem fold. With pinking shears, cut the top edge ¼ inch narrower than the hem. Insert the shaped webbing between the hem and the garment, and *steam-press to fuse.* Add soft padding to the ironing board, and from the right side of the garment, again *steam-press to fuse.*

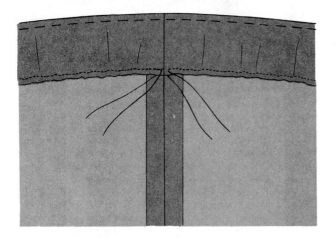

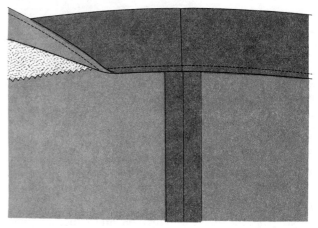

Pants Hems, Plain

Try on the pants, and have someone mark the length at the center front and center back. Remove the pants, turn them wrong side out, and turn up the bottom of the legs on the center-front and center-back markings. Find the hem-fold line on each side of the legs by creasing a straight fold from the center-front marking to the center-back marking. The hem-fold line will slant downward approximately $\frac{1}{4}$ inch from the center front to the center back. Pin and press the hem fold. Work over a sleeve board to measure, mark, and cut the hem width.

Follow the same procedure for finishing pants hems as described for a straight hem on page 37.

Pants Hems, Cuffed

Try on the pants, and have someone mark the length of the pants at the center front and center back. Remove the pants, and turn them wrong side out. Find the length line on each side of the leg by temporarily turning up the bottom of the leg on the center-front and center-back markings. Make a crease from the center-front to the center-back markings, and mark this crease with basting stitches [A]. Then turn down the bottom of the pants leg.

From the basting, measure downward the width of the cuff. Mark and baste a fold line, which will become the top of the cuff. Fold and pin; then baste $\frac{1}{4}$ inch from the cuff fold. Press the fold [B].

Pin the loose part of the cuff to the pants along the line that marks the length of the pants [A] and baste [C]. This basting line will become the bottom of the cuff.

To determine where to cut off the excess length, measure from [C], then mark a line at [D] three quarters of the width of the cuff. Cut off the excess length of the pants leg on this line.

Working over a sleeve board with the cuff turned down, cut fusible webbing as wide as the measurement from [C] to [D], and insert it between the layers. ***Steam-press to fuse.***

The edges of the fused area will be on the inside of the pants. The outside of the fused area will be shielded by the turned-up cuff.

Turn up the cuff, and hand-tack the turned-up cuff to the pants at the center front, the center back, and at each seam. Use a short French tack, placed about $\frac{1}{4}$ inch below the top fold of the cuff.

Remove the bastings and give the pants a final pressing.

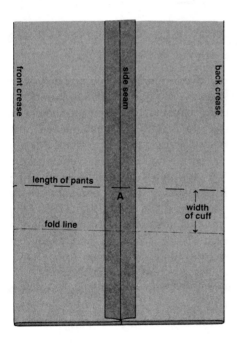

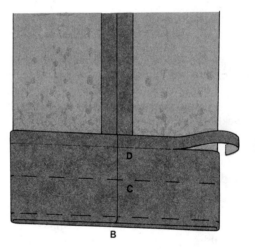

fusibles

IN FASHION DRESSMAKING

If fashion dressmaking takes up most of your sewing time, you must be aware of the many new and unusual high-fashion fabrics that are available. Although these newcomers are beautiful to look at, some of them pose problems when they are being stitched or steam-pressed for shaping.

Fusing an interfacing to some of the new fabrics can simplify construction significantly, especially when the fabric resists penetration by a hand-sewing needle. And for seams that are not smooth and sharp-looking,

if you use fusible webbing to supplement the usual pressing, you will find that many of your problems will be solved.

To keep abreast of the times, and to meet the challenge of these man-made fabrics, new sewing methods and products have been developed, but they must be used correctly. This chapter describes new methods for treating darts, collars, hems, and dressmaker details that could resist your efforts if you used conventional sewing procedures.

FUSIBLE WEBBING FOR PROBLEM SEAMS

Although there are four different methods for treating seams and darts with fusible webbing, the texture of the fashion fabric and the results of your swatch tests will quickly determine the method that is best. *Caution:* All garment fitting and the pressing of all seams and darts must be completed *before* you begin to fuse.

Opened Seam Allowances
Fused to Garment

This method is suitable only for suedelike, bonded, and other thick, crease-resistant fabrics; a fused seam

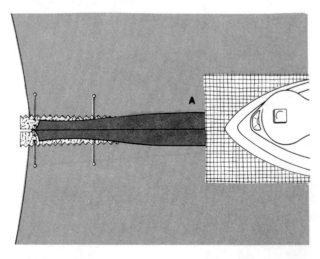

allowance on thin fabrics would probably show a line or a shadow on the outside of the garment.

On straight seams, first press the seam as stitched, then press the seam allowances open. Do not finish the seam edges unless the fabric ravels. For each seam allowance, cut a strip of fusible webbing $\frac{1}{8}$ inch narrower than the seam allowance. Pink the outside edges of the webbing strips to prevent the seam edges from embossing a line on the outside of the fashion fabric when they are pressed. Insert a strip of webbing under each seam allowance, and pin if necessary. Spot-fuse the seam allowances open between the pins. Remove the pins, cut off the webbing that extends beyond the end of the seam, and *steam-press to fuse* [A].

For curved seams, the procedure is the same as for straight seams except in cutting the webbing. Instead of cutting curved strips of webbing to follow the curved seam allowances, cut a straight strip of fusible webbing $\frac{1}{8}$ inch narrower than each seam allowance, and pink one edge of each strip. Every half inch or so, slash the webbing from the pinked edge almost to the straight edge. The slashes will allow the webbing to conform to the curve of the seam, separating on the outside of the curve, and overlapping on the inside of the curve. Follow the same spot-fusing and fusing procedure as for straight seams [B].

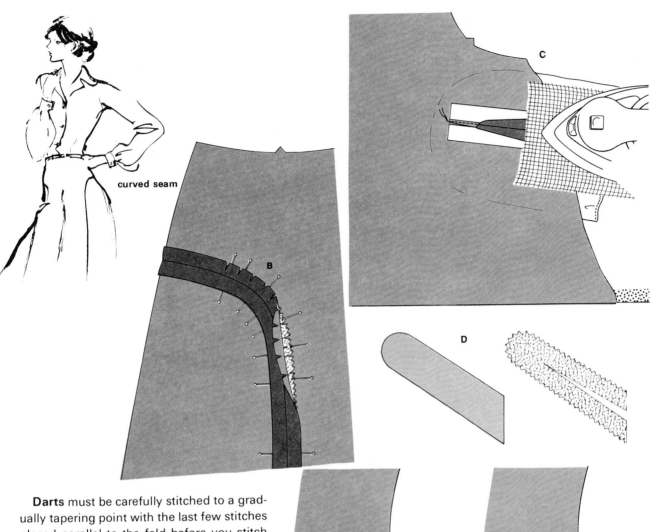

curved seam

Darts must be carefully stitched to a gradually tapering point with the last few stitches placed parallel to the fold before you stitch off the fold. Leave the thread ends about three inches long so that they can be tied into a single knot. Press the stitching to embed it into the fabric and to smooth the seam. Slash along the dart fold, stopping as near the point as possible without weakening the dart. Insert strips of paper under the cut edges. Press the dart open over a press mitt [C]; then discard the strips of paper.

Cut a strip of fusible webbing $\frac{3}{8}$ inch wider than the two pressed-open seam allowances and 1 inch longer than the dart. Round the corners at one end of the strip, and slash through the center from the other end almost as far as the dart point. Pink the outer edges. Cut a piece of underlining or a piece of thin lining fabric the same shape, length and width, but do not slash through the center [D].

Insert the fusible webbing under the allowances, letting it extend beyond the point of the dart. Place the lining over the webbing, and spot-fuse to hold the layers in place [E]. Working over a press mitt, **steam-press to fuse** [F]; then lightly press the dart from the right side.

If the dart has been stitched so that it has a gradually tapering point, the fused lining at and beyond the point will prevent the fabric from dimpling, and the garment will be shaped smoothly. A dart that has been stitched so that it has a blunted point will develop a deep dimple or wrinkle in the garment fabric; this cannot be pressed out.

Open Seam Allowances
Fused to Underlining

Some fabrics, especially those that are sheer or have a shiny surface, will show a difference in texture wherever seam allowances have been fused directly to them. Unfortunately, the seam allowances will not stay pressed open unless they are fused, and as a result, the seam will draw. An underlining is usually the solution to this problem because it provides an alternative surface to which the seam allowances can be fused.

Cut the underlining by the same pattern as the fashion fabric. Hand-baste the underlining and the fashion fabric together at the center of each section and within each seam allowance. Assemble the garment sections, treating the fabric and the underlining as one layer.

For straight seams, stitch the seams, and trim the underlining seam allowances to $\frac{1}{4}$ inch. Cut $\frac{1}{2}$-inch-wide strips of fusible webbing, and insert a strip under each seam allowance [A]. ***Steam-press to fuse.***

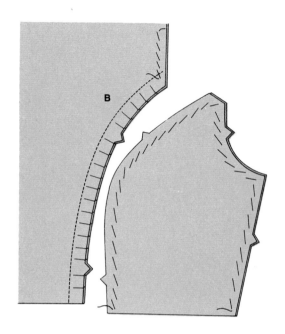

Working over a press mitt, press the curved seam allowances open. Trim the underlining seam allowances to $\frac{1}{4}$ inch. Trim the fashion fabric seam allowances to one-half width. Cut strips of fusible webbing $\frac{1}{4}$ inch wide for each seam allowance. Working over a press mitt, insert a strip of webbing under each seam allowance, and spot-fuse only a few inches at a time. When the entire seam allowance has been spot-fused, ***steam-press to fuse*** [C].

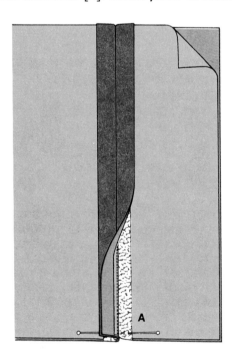

For curved seams, such as the modified princess seam, place stay stitching a scant $\frac{5}{8}$ inch from the edge of the inside curve of the seam line. Slash into the seam allowance at $\frac{1}{2}$-inch intervals so that it will be able to spread and conform to the seam allowance of the outside curve as you stitch the seam; stitch inside the stay stitching [B].

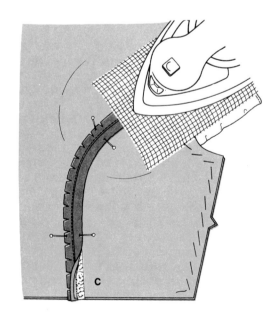

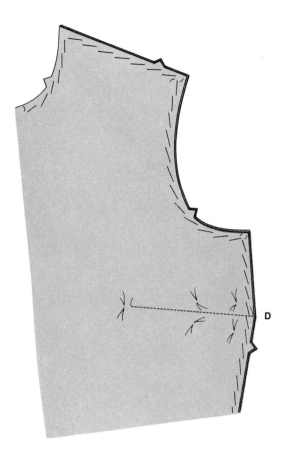

Darts that are made through both the underlining and the fashion fabric are more accurate when a line of stay stitching is placed through the center at the dart fold line [D]. The stay stitching should extend almost to the point of the dart. Fold, pin, and stitch the dart from the wide end to the point, tapering the point gradually and placing the last few stitches parallel to the fold before you stitch off the fold. Leave the thread ends about 3 inches long so that they can be tied into a single knot.

Slash the dart below the stay stitching, almost to the point. Trim both seam allowances on the underneath half of the dart to ¼ inch. The two layers of fabric are held together by the stay stitching on the top half of the dart [E]. Working over a press mitt, press the dart carefully.

Cut a wedge-shaped piece of fusible webbing, and insert it under the top allowance. Working over a press mitt, *steam-press to fuse* [F].

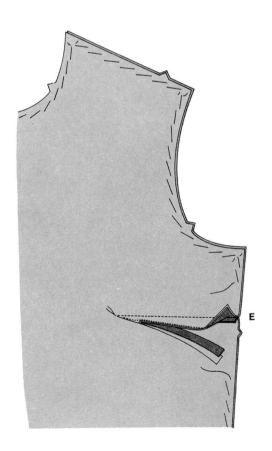

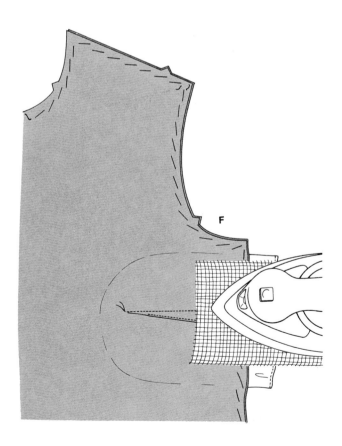

Opened Seam Allowances
Fused to a Stay

Fusing a stay to opened seam allowances with fusible webbing is another way to treat seams so that they will look sharply pressed without having to apply fusible webbing to the wrong side of the fashion fabric.

There are many variations of this method, so choose the one that meets the requirements of your fashion fabric. For example, on heavyweight or thick fabrics the seam allowances may be held open with fusible webbing and a stay of thin lining or underlining fabric to avoid excessive bulk. On medium-weight or lightweight silklike fabrics, the stay may be either of self-fabric or of a lighter-weight fabric. Remember, do not fuse seam allowances open until after all fitting and careful pressing of each seam has been completed.

For straight seams, press the seam allowances open. Choose from a lightweight lining, lightweight underlining, or self-fabric, and cut a piece of the fabric either on the straight grain or on the true bias the combined width of the two seam allowances (usually 1¼ inches). Cut a piece of fusible webbing the same width, and place it on top of the pressed-open seam allowances. Place the stay on top of the webbing, and spot-fuse; then ***steam-press to fuse.***

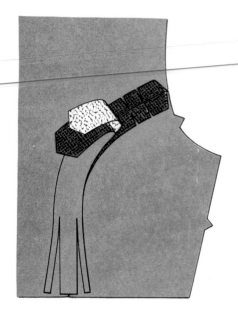

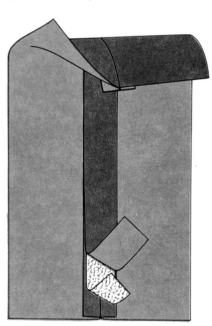

If the fabric ravels, trim ⅛ inch from each seam allowance edge. On most fabrics the cut edges will not ravel because the fabric yarns will be held in place by the fused webbing.

For curved seams, clip and notch the seam allowances so that they will press flat. On the pattern piece for the inside curve, draw a line 1¼ inches inside the cutting line, and cut a stay following the line you just drew. Cut a piece of fusible webbing the same shape as the stay. Position the webbing on top of the seam allowances, cover the webbing with the stay, and pin

the layers in place. Spot-fuse between the pins; then, remove the pins, and ***steam-press to fuse.***

Trim ⅛ to ¼ inch from the seam allowance edges to reduce bulk. *Remember:* Press carefully over a press mitt to obtain the shaping that a curved seam is designed to give a garment.

The stay for a curved seam may be cut from fabric on the true bias also, but it should be cut a little wider than 1¼ inches. Using an iron, shape the bias strip into a curve. The strip will become narrower as it is ironed into shape.

Darts should be carefully stitched to a tapering point, threads tied into a single knot, and pressed over a press mitt. Slash open the dart on the crease, and press the allowances open. Cut triangular pieces of fusible webbing and fabric that match the shape of the dart. Position the webbing on top of the opened allowances, cover the webbing with the fabric, and ***steam-press to fuse.***

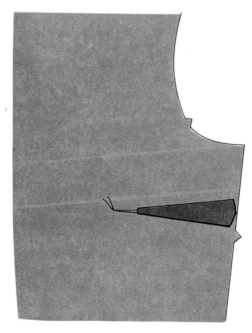

For armhole seams in raglan sleeves, the portion from the neckline to the front and back notches should be treated the same way as opened straight seams that are fused to a stay; the underarm portion should be reinforced with stitching placed $\frac{1}{16}$ inch outside the stitching on the seam line. Slash the seam allowances at the notches, almost to the reinforcing stitches. At the underarm, stitch again through both seam allowances $\frac{1}{4}$ inch outside the armhole stitching; then, cut off the part of the seam allowances that extends beyond the stitching line.

Unopened Seam Allowances
Fused Together

All nylon and polyester silklike woven fabrics ravel excessively, and cannot be pressed sharply enough for their seams to have a neat, finished appearance. Although French seams could be used with these fabrics, the several rows of stitching tend to increase puckering. Using mock-French seams will result in greatly diminished raveling and puckering, and you will have a better-looking garment overall.

Mock-French seams are made by stitching a plain seam, fusing the seam allowances together, and then trimming the seam allowances to $\frac{3}{8}$ inch.

Remember, before fusing, make sure that the garment fits properly. After fusing, press the seam allowances toward the front on shoulder and underarm seams. Press all vertical darts toward the center front or center back. Press horizontal darts or seam allowances downward. Press ungathered sleeve and armhole seam allowances toward the sleeve, and press gathered sleeve and armhole seam allowances toward the bodice.

For straight seams, press the seam allowances together as stitched to embed the stitching; then cut a straight-edged strip of fusible webbing $\frac{1}{2}$ inch wide, and insert it between the seam allowances close to the stitching [A]. First, spot-fuse; then, ***steam-press to fuse.*** Trim the seam allowances to $\frac{3}{8}$-inch width.

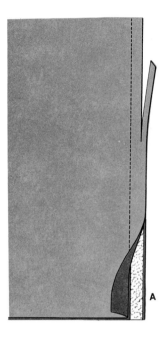

For curved seams, press the seam allowances together as stitched to embed the stitching; then cut a strip of fusible webbing $\frac{1}{2}$ inch wide, and insert it between the seam allowances close to the stitching [B]. If necessary, slash the outside edge of the webbing to allow it to conform to the curve of the seam. First, spot-fuse; then, **steam-press to fuse.** Trim the seam allowances to $\frac{3}{8}$-inch width.

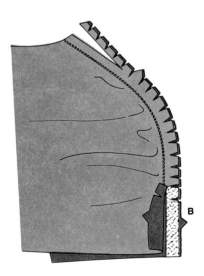

Darts are handled the same way as seams. Stitch the dart to a gradually tapering point, tie the thread ends into a single knot, and press the dart over a press mitt. Slash the dart open along the crease line. Cut a wedge-shaped piece of fusible webbing, and insert it between the dart allowances. Working over a press mitt, place a piece of plain paper between the dart and the garment to prevent the fusible resin from oozing onto the garment fabric. *Steam-press to fuse* [C]. Trim the edges of the dart just enough to remove any raveling.

Armhole seams in set-in sleeves must be made properly if you are going to use mock-French seams. If the set-in sleeve is designed to have a smooth, ungathered look, control the fullness in the sleeve cap between the front and back notches with *one* row of ease stitching, placed a scant $\frac{5}{8}$ inch from the seam edge. Pin the sleeve into the armhole, matching the underarm seams, the shoulder seam with the marking for the top of the sleeve cap, the front notches, the back notches, and the pattern markings for the placement of ease in the front and back of the sleeve cap.

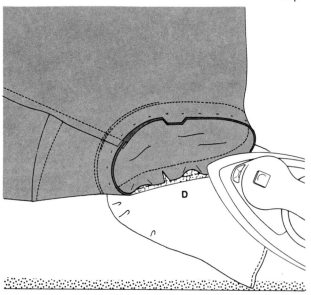

Draw the bobbin thread of the ease stitching to make the sleeve fit the armhole at the seam line, distributing the ease equally. Baste if necessary.

Stitch just inside the ease stitching, taking a full $\frac{5}{8}$ inch seam allowance. Stitch from the sleeve side so that you can see the ease stitching. At the bottom of the armhole, stitch just outside the seam line from notch to notch to reinforce the seam; then remove the ease stitching.

Working over a press mitt, press the armhole seam just to the stitching line, not into the sleeve cap.

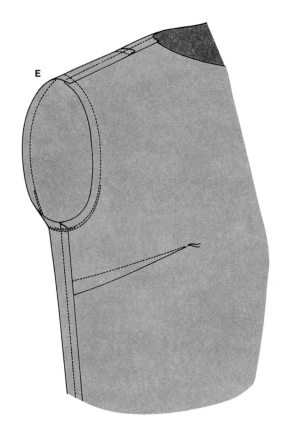

To fuse the seam allowances together, choose one of the two following methods:

1. Cut strips of fusible webbing that are 2 inches long and $\frac{1}{2}$ inch wide. Insert and spot-fuse one strip at a time between the seam allowances. After the armhole seam allowances have been spot-fused entirely, *steam-press to fuse.* Trim the seam allowances to $\frac{3}{8}$ inch, and turn the seam allowance into the armhole.

2. Using fusible webbing yardage, cut the webbing by the armhole front and back pattern pieces $\frac{5}{8}$ inch wide. Insert the webbing between the seam allowances, and hand-baste the webbing to the armhole seam allowance.

Working over a press mitt, spot-fuse the seam allowances together from the sleeve side, spot-fusing only a small area at one time [D]. Then, with the armhole side up, *steam-press to fuse.* Trim seam allowance to one-half width [E] and turn allowance toward sleeve.

For a gathered sleeve cap place two rows of stitching over the cap before you stitch the sleeve seam. With the right side of the sleeve up, place the first row of stitching a scant $\frac{5}{8}$ inch from the seam edge, and the second row $\frac{1}{4}$ inch outside the first row. Stitch the sleeve seam, fuse the seam allowances, and apply the cuff. Refer to pages 58 and 59.

Draw the bobbin threads in the sleeve cap, and distribute the fullness evenly. Pin and baste the sleeve into the armhole, matching seams and pattern markings. Stitch just inside the first line of gathering stitches. Reinforce the bottom of the armhole from notch to notch. Keeping the seam allowances together as stitched, press the seam allowances and the armhole stitching [F].

Cut shaped pieces of fusible webbing by the front and back armhole patterns. Remove the gathering stitches that are nearest to the seam line, but *do not* remove the stitches that are nearest to the seam edge. Insert the webbing between the seam allowances, and hand-baste the webbing to the armhole seam allowance. Spot-fuse; then ***steam-press to fuse*** [G]. Trim the seam allowances to $\frac{3}{8}$ inch; turn seam allowances toward the bodice.

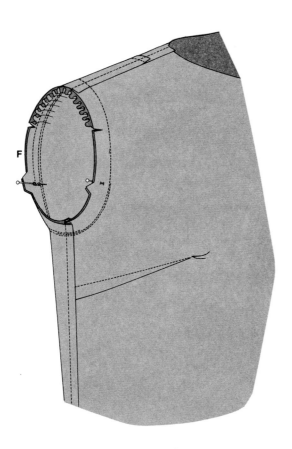

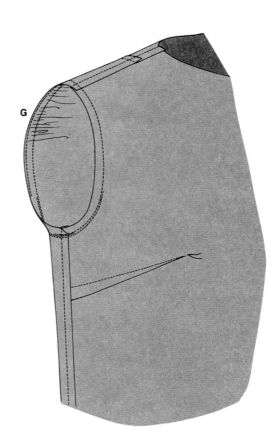

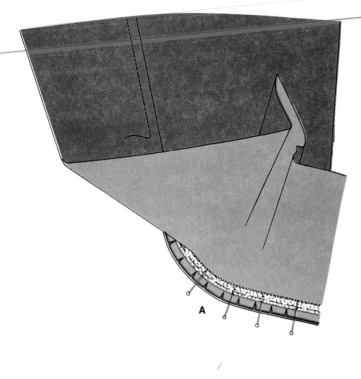

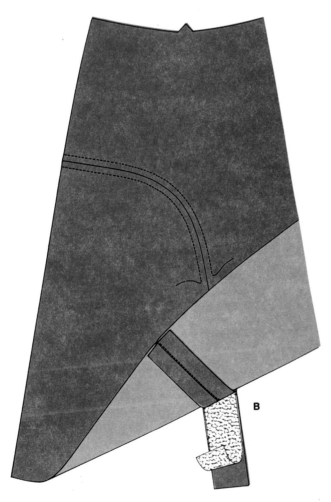

Applying fusible webbing between seam layers prevents the fabric from shifting or feeding unevenly when seams are topstitched. Although some soft, lightweight fabrics are not suitable for this method of treating seams, most topstitched seams will show improvement if they are treated in one of the ways that follow.

Plain Welt Seams

For curved seams, stay-stitch a scant $\frac{5}{8}$ inch from the seam edge of the inside curve, and slash from the seam edge almost to the stay stitching. Omit the stay stitching for straight seams.

Stitch a plain seam $\frac{5}{8}$ inch from the edge, letting the slashes open to conform to the curve of the other seam edge. Press the seam allowances together as stitched to embed the stitches; then press the seam allowances only in one direction to prepare them for topstitching.

Pin and hand-baste a $\frac{3}{8}$-inch-wide strip of fusible webbing to the seam allowance that lies against the garment. On the curves, slash partway through the webbing at intervals so that the webbing will conform to the curves [A].

First, **steam-press to fuse.** Then, topstitch $\frac{3}{8}$ inch from the seam line. Do *not* attempt to remove the basting; it has been fused to the seam allowance.

Center-stitched Plain Welt Seams

Prepare this seam the same way as a plain welt seam, except press the seam allowances open, and slash the outside curve of the seam allowance at $\frac{1}{2}$ inch intervals to within $\frac{1}{8}$ inch of the stitching so that the seam allowance will lie flat. If the slashes overlap, trim the edges so they just touch.

By the pattern, cut $1\frac{1}{4}$-inch-wide strips of fabric and fusible webbing that conform to the shape of the pressed-open seam allowances. Place the webbing over the seam allowances, position the strips of fabric over the webbing, and pin in place. Spot-fuse between the pins; then remove the pins. From the right side, **steam-press to fuse.** Place a row of topstitching $\frac{3}{8}$ inch from each side of the seam line [B].

Faced Welt Seams

By the pattern, cut a $1\frac{1}{4}$-inch-wide shaped facing for the inside curve (upper side) of the seam. Stitch the facing on the seam line, taking a $\frac{5}{8}$-inch seam allowance. Trim the seam allowances to $\frac{3}{8}$ inch, and slash them from the edge to within $\frac{1}{8}$ inch of the stitching at $\frac{1}{2}$-inch intervals. Press to embed the stitching; then press the seam allowances open. Turn the facing to the wrong side; baste if necessary. Press the edge so that it favors the outside.

To prepare the underneath seam, cut a ½-inch-wide strip of fusible webbing that conforms to the shape of the seam allowance, and stitch the webbing to the seam allowance ⅛ inch from the edge [C]. Pin the seam layers together, and hand-baste about ⅜ inch from the faced edge. Spot-fuse between the pins; then, remove the pins, and **steam-press to fuse.**

Topstitch ⅜ inch from the faced edge. Remove the hand basting in short segments while the fabric is still warm from the steam pressing.

Slot Seams

Although it is not necessary to face a straight slot seam, a curved slot seam must be faced even if only a part of the seam is curved. By the pattern, cut a shaped facing and a strip of self-fabric for an underlay 1¼ to 1½ inches wide for both seam edges.

Stitch a facing to each seam edge, taking a ⅝-inch seam allowance. Trim all seam allowances to ⅜-inch

width. Slash or notch the curved portions so that the seam allowances will lie flat and serve as a filler for the part of the seam detail that extends beyond the top-stitching. Press the stitching; then press the seam allowances open.

Turn the facings to the wrong side, and press them sharply on the stitching line. Hand-baste through both the garment and the facing, ⅜ inch from the seam edges, and press. Catch-stitch the faced edges together [D].

Turn the garment section wrong side up on an ironing board, and pin ⅜-inch-wide strips of fusible webbing to the facing edges. Slash partway into the webbing to allow it to conform to the curves. Place the self-fabric underlay over the webbing on each seam allowance, and spot-fuse between the pins. Remove the pins, and **steam-press to fuse.**

Topstitch ⅜ inch from each faced edge. Remove the basting and catch stitching; then press to embed the stitching. Trim the edges of the seam allowances to remove raveling or unevenness.

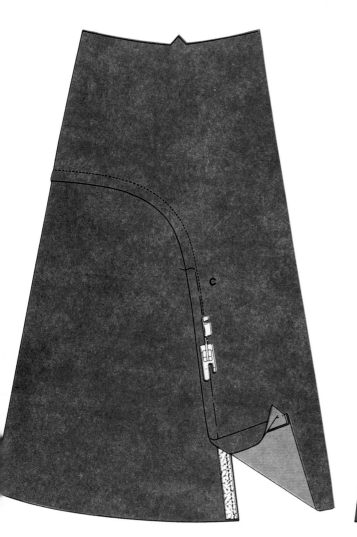

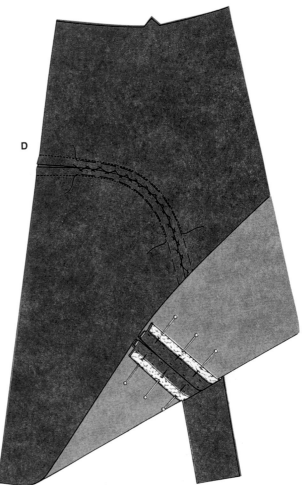

DRESSMAKER TECHNIQUES FOR CLOSED COLLARS

The current fashion trend, as well as the pattern design and the fashion fabric, determines how much firmness, shaping, and loft a collar should have. Sometimes fashion dictates a crisp, firm look; at other times, a soft, unstructured look. There are times when the fabric alone has enough body to support itself; at other times the fabric needs interfacing to give it support, shape, or loft.

As a rule, an appropriate interfacing or interlining will improve the appearance of a collar if the requirements of all three elements—fabric, pattern design, and fashion—are taken into consideration. To help make your choice, take the fabrics that you intend to use in the collar and drape them in layers over one hand. Feel them as if they were one layer of fabric to determine whether or not the combined layers will have the required characteristics for your collar when it has been completed. Keep in mind that fusible interfacing has more body after it has been fused.

To be able to meet the varying needs of all the different fabrics, patterns, and fashions, you should know many ways to interface a collar.

Under Collar, Fusible Interfacing

The conventional way to interface a collar is to apply the interfacing to the under collar. This method is appropriate for medium-weight fabrics, and one of the three fusible interfacings that follow would be a good choice for this purpose. Easy-Shaper[3] Light Weight by Stacy and Stylus Fusible Uni-Stretch[1] Light Weight by Armo are stable lengthwise and give crosswise. FuseAKnit[1] is a luxurious nylon knit with a fusible resin backing.[†]

Cut the upper collar, the under collar, and the interfacing by the same pattern. Lightly fuse the interfacing to the wrong side of the under collar, keeping the iron away from the seam allowances along the outer edges so that they will be very lightly fused. With right sides together, pin the upper collar to the under collar, and using a seam guide set at an angle to keep the seam allowances even, stitch on the seam line. Pivot the

collar on the index finger of your left hand when stitching around the curve [A].

Lightly press the seam allowances and stitching; then, with your fingertips, loosen the fusible interfacing over the seam allowances close to the stitching, and trim the seam allowances of the under collar $\frac{1}{4}$ inch from the stitching. Notch the trimmed seam allowances as shown in [B]. From the interfacing side, **_steam-press to fuse._** Make sure that the interfacing is completely fused to the under collar.

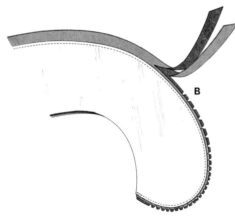

Finger-press the seam allowances open so that the collar will turn sharply on the seam [C]. Sometimes it may be necessary to use an iron and a seam board to press the seam allowances open.

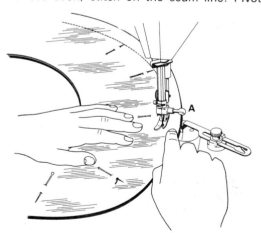

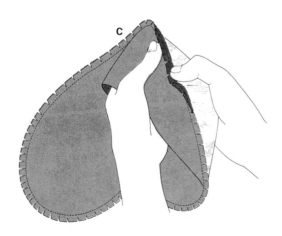

†Numbers indicate owners of registered or trademark names, as shown on page 5.

With the collar turned wrong side out, understitch through the under collar, interfacing, and all seam allowances [D].

Turn the collar right side out, and press the turned edges. Then, shape the collar to form a roll at the neckline. Place pins to hold the layers in place as they will be when the collar is rolled. Depending on the thickness of the collar, the seam allowances of the under collar and interfacing will extend beyond the seam allowance of the upper collar; on heavier fabrics the seam allowances will extend farther.

Stay-stitch a scant $5/8$ inch from the neckline edge of the under collar, and clip into the seam allowances to make it easier to apply the collar to the garment [E].

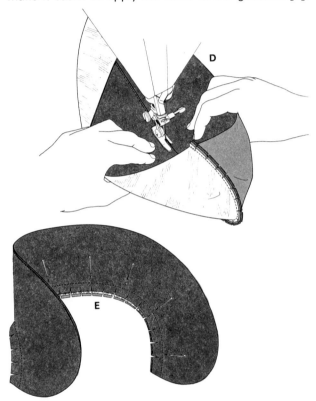

Upper Collar, Fusible Interfacing

In collars made of soft, lightweight fabrics such as polyester crepe, nylon tricot, or nylon surah, the interfacing should be fused to the wrong side of the upper collar instead of to the under collar. Either FuseAKnit[1] by Armo, or Easy-Shaper[3] Light Weight by Stacy are effective in giving soft shaping. By fusing the interfacing to the wrong side of the upper collar, the seam allowances on the inside of the finished collar will fall behind the interfacing, giving a smooth surface to the top of the collar.

Follow the steps outlined above for making the collar, except fuse the interfacing to the wrong side of the upper collar instead of to the under collar. Usually the understitching can be omitted, and because the fabric layers are thin, the neckline edges will be even when the collar is rolled. Topstitching may be added around the outer edge, or the edge may remain plain.

Upper Collar and Under Collar, Fusible Interfacing

Fusible interfacing is especially appropriate for loosely structured knit or woven fabrics made of polyester, acrylic, and nylon fibers or for blends of these fibers with rayon or natural fibers. Fusing the interfacing to both collar sections adds stability to the collar and sharpness to the turned edge. For this method it is important to use a very lightweight, fusible interfacing, such as Easy-Shaper[3] Light Weight by Stacy. Follow the procedure described above, except fuse the interfacing to both collar layers. Omit the understitching, but add topstitching if desired.

Underlined Upper Collar, Fusible Webbing Along Seam

With soft fabrics, the soft look is achieved by underlining the upper collar with self-fabric or with a lightweight underlining fabric, and then stitching a shaped piece of fusible webbing into the seam next to the underlining as shown [F].

Cut three fabric sections and one fusible webbing section by the pattern. Place the layers one on top of the other in the following order from the top down:

> fusible webbing
> underlining
> upper collar, wrong side up
> under collar, right side up

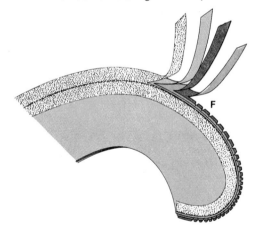

Pin, then stitch $5/8$ inch from the edge. Cut away the fusible webbing $3/8$ inch *inside* the stitching line; then cut away the webbing barely to the *outside* of the stitching line. Trim the underlining to $1/8$ inch; the upper collar to $1/4$ inch, and the under collar to $3/8$ inch. Cut notches into the seam allowances at the curves.

Turn the collar right side out, and finger-press the seam allowances open. Be careful to turn the layers so that the seam allowances lie between the underlining and the under collar. With your fingertips, work the edges until the turn is smooth; then lightly press the edges. ***Steam-press to fuse.***

Do not understitch; use topstitching for an accent if desired.

DRESSMAKER TECHNIQUES FOR OPEN COLLARS, LAPELS, AND FRONT CLOSURES

When the conventional method is used to interface a dress or a blouse having an open collar, lapels, and a front closure, the interfacing is applied to the wrong sides of the under collar and front sections. This method works well with medium-weight fabrics and lightweight, nonwoven, fusible interfacing, but lightweight fabrics must be handled in a different way to prevent the seam allowances and the unstitched edge of the front interfacing from showing.

The conventional method and alternative procedures for applying interfacing follow.

Applying Interfacing,
Conventional Method

Cut lightweight, nonwoven, fusible interfacing by the patterns for the under collar and the front facing. Remove the seam allowance from the inside edge of each front interfacing. Transfer the significant pattern markings to the interfacing, such as the dot markings that indicate the end of the collar stitching and the end of the lapel stitching.

Steam-press the collar sections, the fronts, and the front facings. Place the interfacing on the wrong side of the under collar, and lightly steam-press, keeping the tip of the iron inside the seam lines along the edge of the collar so that you do not fuse the seam allowances to the under collar.

Place the front interfacing on the wrong side of each front section, and steam-press to lightly fuse, keeping the tip of the iron inside the seam lines along the front edge. Keeping right sides together, pin the interfaced under collar to the upper collar; then pin each interfaced front to the front facing.

Stitch the collar unit $\frac{5}{8}$ inch from the edge, starting and stopping the stitching at the pattern markings. Backstitch at the pattern dot markings that indicate the end of the collar [A].

Lift the edge of the interfacing from the seam allowances, and trim away the interfacing close to the stitching. Trim the collar and front seam allowances to unequal widths: the under collar to $\frac{1}{8}$ inch; the upper collar to $\frac{1}{4}$ inch; the lapel front to $\frac{1}{8}$ inch; the lapel facing to $\frac{1}{4}$ inch; the rest of the front facing below the first button to $\frac{1}{8}$ inch; and the remainder of the garment front to $\frac{1}{4}$ inch [B]. By making the seam allowances wider when they are next to the most visible side of the collar, you are following the rule for trimming enclosed seam allowances to unequal widths.

To remove bulk, cut narrow notches into the seam allowances at the curves, spacing the notches evenly and close together.

While the interfaced sections are still flat, place them one at a time on an ironing board with the interfacing up. Taking care to avoid fusing the neckline seam allowance to the front section, *steam-press to fuse.*

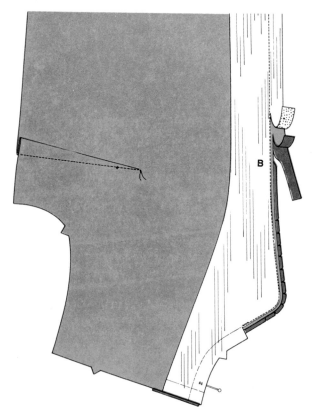

Working over a seam board, and using the tip of the iron, press open the trimmed seam allowances of the collar. Turn the collar right side out, finger-pressing the seam line to form a sharp fold.

If it is necessary to hold the edge in place until it can be pressed, hand-baste along the edge, using diagonal basting stitches. Press the collar, favoring the single layer that is the upper collar. Clip ½ inch into the seam allowance of the upper collar at the markings that indicate the position of the shoulder seam. Turn the seam allowance between the clips to the inside and edge-stitch [C].

Clip through the seam allowances of each front and facing at the dot that indicates end of the collar [D]. Press open the lapel and front seam allowances, and turn each section right side out. Finger-press, and hand-baste if necessary. Press the lapel, favoring the facing side; then press below the top button, favoring the front side.

Stitch the shoulder seams, catching the interfacing in the seam. Press the seam allowances open. Trim the interfacing outside the seam line stitching. (If the pattern has a back facing, join the facing shoulder seams, press the seam allowances open and trim to one-half width. If the pattern does not have a back facing, finish the inside facing edge with machine overedging or with straight edgestitching.)

To prepare the neckline for attaching the collar, stay-stitch ½ inch from the seam edge from one dot marking on the lapel, around the back to the other dot marking [D]. Trim the corners of the shoulder seam allowances at the neckline; then, stay-stitch the neckline of the facing.

To attach the under collar to the blouse, pin at the center back, shoulders and fronts, keeping the collar seam allowance folded back where the collar meets the lapel [E]. The collar will appear to be larger than the neckline. Clip into the neckline seam allowance at about ½-inch intervals, almost to the stay stitching, to relieve the curved seam allowance of the neckline so that it will fit the collar. If necessary, baste. Stitch from the center back to each end of the collar. Overlap the stitching at the center back [F] and tie the threads.

To attach the upper collar to the facings, pin each front part of the upper collar to a front of the neckline facing [G]. Clip the neckline seam allowances. Stitch

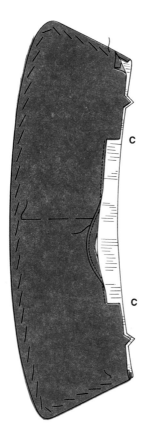

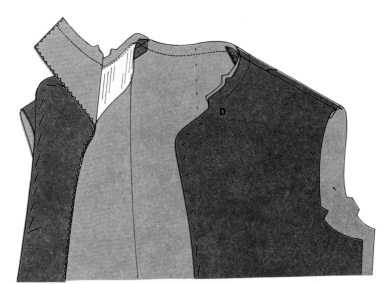

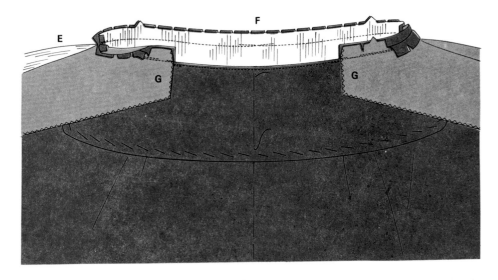

the seams according to the pattern markings, and backstitch or tie the thread ends.

Press all seam allowances open. Trim seam allowances to $\frac{1}{4}$-inch width, and press again.

To tack the seam allowances of the lapel and upper collar to the seam allowances of the garment and under collar, you can use either a short tacking or catch stitch that alternates between layers [H], or you can use a $\frac{1}{2}$-inch-wide strip of fusible webbing. Baste the webbing to the lower seam allowances [I]. Then, carefully pin the upper seam allowances over them. Spot-fuse between the pins. Remove the pins and **steam-press to fuse.**

Slip-stitch the edge-stitched portion across the back of the upper collar to the neckline seam allowance that turns into the collar.

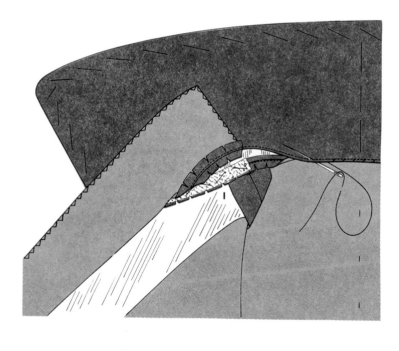

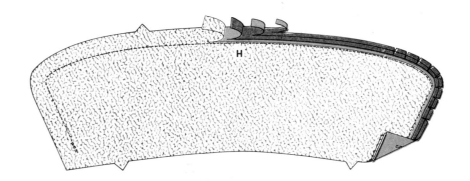

Self-fabric Interfacing, Plus Fusible Webbing

This method is good for a blouse, a bodysuit, or a soft shirtwaist style made of nylon tricot or Qiana* nylon. Fusing a layer of self-fabric to the wrong side of the under collar and lapel in a way that entraps the seam allowances keeps the edges neatly turned, and adds a little body to the collar and lapels.

Cut three collar sections of the fashion fabric and cut one section of fusible webbing. Lay them one on top of the other in the following order: self-fabric interfacing, right side up; upper collar, right side up; under collar, wrong side up; fusible webbing. Stitch from one neckline seam line marking to the other, stitching around the outside of the collar. Backstitch at both ends. Trim the seam allowances as follows: fusible webbing, trim outside the stitching; under collar, to $\frac{1}{16}$ inch; upper collar, to $\frac{1}{8}$ inch; self-fabric interfacing to $\frac{1}{4}$ inch [H].

Notch the seam allowances around curves, and clip off the seam allowance of the interfacing for $\frac{3}{4}$ inch at the neckline. Do not press yet.

Lift and turn the bottom layer (the interfacing) over the fusible webbing to entrap the seam allowances. Working from the center back toward each end, and from the seam edge toward the neckline, *steam-press to fuse.* Then, lift and turn the upper collar over the interfacing and press the edges. To make sure that the webbing has been fused completely, *steam-press to fuse* from the under-collar side.

To interface the lapel, cut a paper pattern by the facing pattern for the interfacing and the fusible webbing. Cut off the paper pattern just below the first buttonhole, and cut $\frac{5}{8}$ inch from the inside edge. Cut one piece of webbing and one self-fabric interfacing for each lapel.

Lay the sections one on top of the other in the following order: fusible webbing; blouse front, right side up; blouse facing, wrong side up; self-fabric interfacing, wrong side up. Starting at the bottom edge of the self-fabric interfacing, lay a $\frac{7}{8}$-inch-wide strip of fusible webbing over the seam allowance, and stitch through the webbing as you stitch the seam [I].

On the front, trim off the webbing seam allowance outside the stitching, leaving $\frac{1}{4}$ inch extending over

*Trademark of E. I. Dupont de Nemours & Co.

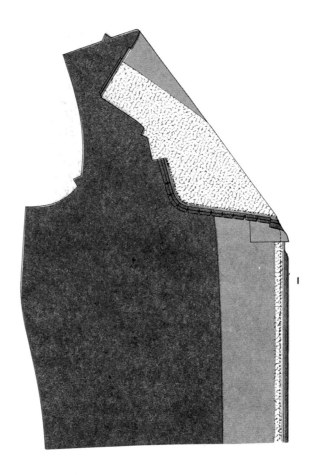

the facing. Trim the front facing seam allowance to $\frac{1}{8}$-inch width, and trim the blouse front seam allowance to $\frac{1}{4}$-inch width.

On the lapels, trim off the webbing seam allowance outside the stitching. Trim the other seam allowances as follows: front, to $\frac{1}{16}$ inch; facing, to $\frac{1}{8}$ inch; interfacing, to $\frac{1}{4}$ inch. Notch the seam allowances around the curves. Lift and turn the interfacing over the webbing to entrap the seam allowances. *Steam-press to fuse.* Then, turn the facing over the fused interfacing on the lapel and over the seam allowances down the front. Steam-press the edges from the right side to sharpen the seam line. Then, from the wrong side, *steam-press to fuse.*

Assemble the garment and attach the collar the same way as described on pages 53 and 54.

Soft Treatment

Use this method for soft, supple shirtwaist styles or wherever an unstructured look is desired. For this method, fusible webbing is used to hold the seam allowances in position, and the faced portion of the blouse is underlined with self-fabric or with thin, regular interfacing.

Refer to page 51, *Underlined Upper Collar, Fusible Webbing Along Seam,* for instructions on assembling the collar. The procedure for this method is the same; you begin and end the collar stitching with backstitches at the neckline seam line.

Handle the lapels and front similarly to the collar. Cut two front facings for each side. Place one front facing over the front with right sides together; then place the other front facing (underlining) on top of the facing. Cut a piece of fusible webbing by the pattern from $\frac{3}{8}$ to 1 inch wider than the width of the seam allowance. Lay the webbing over the underlining, matching all seam edges. Stitch from the lapel marking to the bottom of the front opening, backstitching at both ends.

Trim the lapel seam allowances as follows: underlining, to $\frac{1}{16}$ inch; facing, to $\frac{1}{8}$ inch; blouse front, to $\frac{1}{4}$ inch. Notch the seam allowances at the curve. Trim the front seam allowances a little wider below the first button than the lapel seam allowances: underlining, to $\frac{1}{8}$ inch; facing, to $\frac{1}{4}$ inch; blouse front, to $\frac{3}{8}$ inch. The front seam allowance should be wide enough to cover the strip of webbing when the facing is turned and pressed [J].

To fuse the seam allowances to the underlining on the front below the first button, turn the underlining over the seam allowances and the webbing, and **steam-press to fuse.**

Along the lapel, turn the underlining over against the front, and from the underlining side, **steam-press**

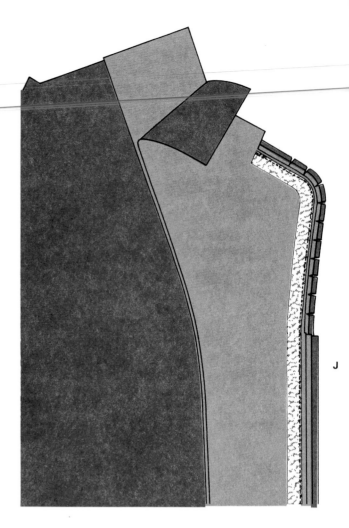

J

to fuse. Turn the facing over to its finished position, and press.

Assemble the blouse in the conventional way, but stitch the front underlining with the facing, and stitch the collar underlining with the upper collar when attaching the collar to the blouse.

DRESSMAKER TECHNIQUES
FOR SLEEVE PLACKETS AND CUFFS

Although cuffs that are applied with a facing can be made the same way as a closed collar, better and easier ways to make a sleeve cuff and placket are described below.

Sleeve Placket, Fusible Interfacing

A sleeve placket that has a dart at the top of the opening in the sleeve and in the facing is the best design with which to use fusible interfacing or webbing. If your pattern does not have a dart in the sleeve placket, create one [A].

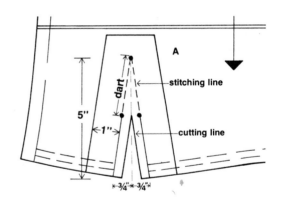

Centered over the area of the sleeve pattern where the cuff ends terminate, draw a line 5 inches long, upward from the bottom sleeve edge and parallel to the lengthwise grain line. At the seam edge, mark a point ¾ inch from each side of this line. With a ruler and a pencil, draw a line from each ¾-inch marking point to the top of the 5-inch centered line, forming a triangle. These lines will serve as stitching lines for the dart and opening of the sleeve placket.

From the edge of the sleeve, draw a line that is parallel to, and ⅜ inch inside, each side of the triangle, stopping where the lines converge. These lines are the cutting lines for the placket opening.

On each stitching line, mark a dot opposite the point where the cutting lines converge. These dots indicate the end of the placket dart. The top of the center line indicates the point of the placket dart. Draw lines 1

inch outside the stitching lines and 1 inch above the top of the dart to serve as cutting lines for the outer edges of the facing.

To make a pattern for the facing and for the fusible interfacing, trace the markings that you have just completed on the sleeve pattern to another piece of paper [B].

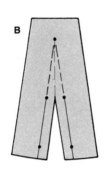

By the facing pattern, cut an interfacing of nonwoven, lightweight, fusible interfacing and a facing for each sleeve. Position the interfacing on the wrong side of the sleeve, fusible side up. Transfer the dart markings to the interfacing. To hold the layers together, machine-stitch from the lower end almost to the point of the dart [C].

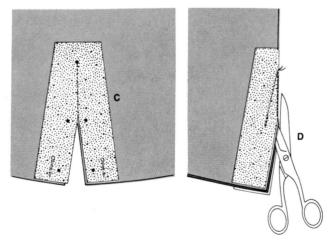

Fold, pin, and stitch the dart from the dot markings to the point. Backstitch at the bottom of the dart, and stitch off and tie the threads at the point of the dart. Slash the dart open on the stitching line [D].

Fold the facing in half with right sides together, and stitch the dart. Slash the facing dart on the fold; then, press the dart open [E]. Pin the facing to the sleeve placket, right sides together. Place a pin at the bottom of the dart, at each side of the placket and at the bottom of each side of the opening, keeping the seam edges together and making sure that the bottoms of the sleeve and facing darts meet.

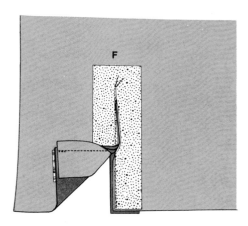

Stitch both sides of the placket, backstitching where the lines of stitching meet. Trim the seam allowances to unequal widths as follows: interfacing, alongside the stitching; sleeve seam allowances, to $\frac{1}{8}$ inch; facing, to $\frac{1}{4}$ inch [F].

Turn the facing to the wrong side, finger-press the darts open, pin, and baste. First, baste the dart stitching lines together, one directly on top of the other, with the seam allowances opened; then, baste the seam edges, favoring the outside of the sleeve [G].

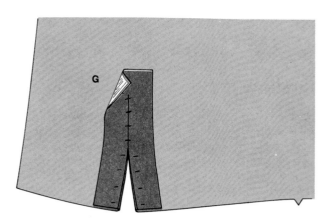

Steam-press to fuse. The interfacing is now fused to the facing, and after the fabrics have cooled, all seam allowances will be held captive between the facing and the interfacing. Finish the placket edges with overedge or zigzag machine stitching, or add lace to the edge.

Sleeve Placket, Self-fabric Underlining and Fusible Webbing

For a soft effect, you may prefer to finish the sleeve placket with a self-fabric underlining and fusible webbing instead of with fusible interfacing.

By the facing pattern, cut one piece of fusible webbing and two pieces of self-fabric for each sleeve. One piece of self-fabric will serve as the underlining; the other piece will serve as the facing.

On the wrong side of the sleeve, place one piece of self-fabric underlining, and cover it with one piece of fusible webbing. Transfer the pattern markings to the webbing. Machine-stitch the center of the dart. Fold, pin, and stitch the dart through all three layers, backstitching at the lower end of the dart, and stitching off the point and tying the thread ends. Slash through the center of the dart.

Pin, stitch, slash open, and press the dart in the facing. Then, pin the facing to the sleeve, right sides together, and stitch the placket sides separately, the same way as for an interfaced placket.

Trim the seam allowances as follows: underlining, to $\frac{1}{16}$ inch; sleeve, to $\frac{1}{8}$ inch; facing, to $\frac{3}{8}$ inch. Turn the facing to the wrong side, and baste the darts together with diagonal basting; baste the edges of the openings, favoring the right side [H].

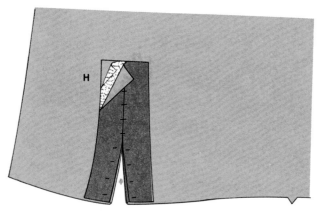

Steam-press to fuse the underlining and facing together. Because the seam allowances are now held captive between the underlining and facing, no further tacking is needed to hold the placket in place. Remove the basting, and finish the edges as desired.

Cuffs, Fusible Interfacing

With most fabrics, nonwoven, lightweight, fusible interfacing produces attractive, supple cuffs. Place the interfacing on the underside of the cuff for a soft look and on the face of the cuff for a crisp look. Let the interfacing extend to the cuff fold at the bottom and to the seam line at the top. *Steam-press to fuse.*

For a soft look, turn the top seam allowance over the interfacing, and edgestitch along the fold [I]. **For a crisp look,** simply turn the seam allowance under, and edgestitch along the fold.

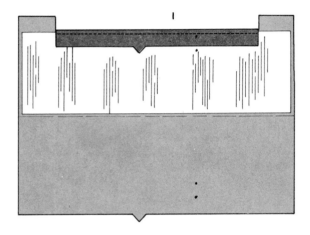

Cuffs, Self-fabric Underlining and Fusible Webbing

An underlining of self-fabric, fused to the underside of the cuff with fusible webbing, gives the cuff body and firmness.

Cut the underlining and fusible webbing so that they extend from the seam line to fold line, and $\frac{1}{2}$ inch from each end [J]. Place the webbing on the underside of the cuff, place the underlining over the webbing, and *steam-press to fuse.* Turn the top seam allowance back over the underlining, and edgestitch the fold.

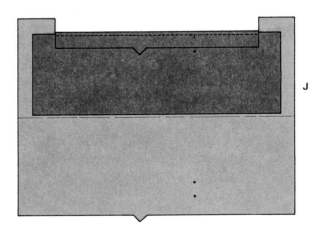

Applying the Cuff

Stitch the underarm sleeve seam; then, press and finish the seam edge. To control the gathers in the bottom of the sleeve, lift and unfold the placket facing so that you can stitch the sleeve without stitching through the facing. Starting at one placket seam, a scant $\frac{5}{8}$ inch from the sleeve edge, stitch around the sleeve to the other placket seam. Make a second row of stitching $\frac{1}{4}$ inch outside the first row.

Draw the threads that lie on the wrong side of the sleeve to form the gathers. With your fingertips, distribute the gathers equally.

With right sides together, pin the face of the cuff to the sleeve. Match all pattern markings, such as the dots that indicate where the cuff meets the underarm sleeve seam and the markings that indicate where the cuff meets the placket seams. Stitch the sleeve to the face of the cuff just inside the control thread. Do not stitch through the placket facings. Either backstitch, or tie the threads at the ends of the stitching lines.

Fold and pin the cuff ends and the short extension beyond the placket. The line of stitching that joins the cuff to the sleeve should meet the line of stitching that closes the end of the cuff.

Trim the seam allowances to uneven widths of $\frac{1}{4}$ and $\frac{3}{8}$ inches, keeping the wider allowance next to the outside layer. Turn the cuff right side out, and slip-stitch the edge-stitched portion of the underside of the cuff to the sleeve along the stitching. Catch the placket facing in the hand stitching.

Use diagonal basting to hold the bottom, top, and edges of the cuff in place [K]. Steam-press; then, remove the basting. Finish with a button and button-hole or with eyelets for cuff links.

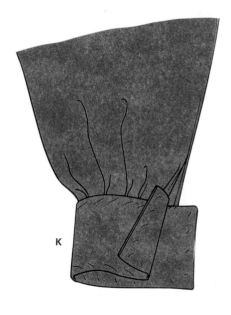

DRESSMAKER TECHNIQUES FOR HEMS

The soft-fold hem and the applied bound-edge hem are dressmaker details that are used in fashion dressmaking.

Soft-fold Hem

The soft-fold hem gives loft and weight to an otherwise thin-looking hem: it is perfect for a soft dress and jacket combination, and it can be made either straight or slightly flared.

Complete the usual steps for preparing a hem, such as measuring the length; pinning and basting the hem fold; pressing the fold; measuring and cutting the hem width; and forming a control thread by stitching from one vertical seam to another, $\frac{1}{4}$ inch from the edge.

With the lengthwise grain perpendicular to the hem length, cut a shaped piece of fusible interfacing $\frac{1}{4}$ inch wider than the hem. Easy-Shaper[3][†] Light Weight by Stacy is an excellent choice for this use. Next, cut a $\frac{1}{2}$- or $\frac{3}{4}$- inch-wide strip of fusible webbing the full length of the hem, and slash from one edge almost to the other at $\frac{1}{2}$-inch intervals so that it will conform to the curve of the hem [A].

With the fusible side down, place the *interfacing* on the wrong side of the garment, letting the interfacing extend $\frac{1}{2}$ inch into the hem fold. **Steam-press to fuse.** Then baste through the hem fold, and press again.

Place the strip of *fusible webbing* along the top edge of the interfacing with the unslashed edge matching the edge of the interfacing [B]. **Steam-press to fuse.**

Except for the top $\frac{1}{4}$ inch, the hem should be fused to the interfacing.

Applied Bound-edge Hem

A wide bound-edge hem may be a decorative feature of a fashion design or it may be used to lengthen a dress that is too short. Although the finished width of the binding may be from $\frac{1}{2}$ to $1\frac{1}{4}$ inches, the width should be kept in proportion to the size of the dress.

From a piece of self-fabric on the true bias, cut a strip of fabric three times the width of the finished binding plus $\frac{5}{8}$ inch. Machine-finish one edge of the bias; then, place the unfinished edge along the hem edge with right sides together. Be careful not to stretch the bias strip. Place pins perpendicular to your intended stitching line, measuring the distance from the edges to keep the seam stitching straight; then, stitch the seam.

From the right side, press the bias strip downward, along the stitching. Carefully turn the bias strip over the wide seam allowances, letting the finished edge extend upward inside the skirt [C]. Baste the hem edge and the top of the bias strip if necessary, and steam-press to shape the bias strip. Take sufficient time with the pressing because it is more of a blocking step than simple pressing. Remove the basting threads.

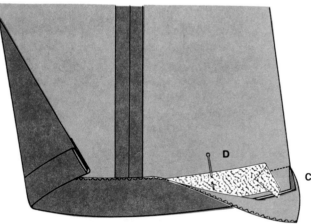

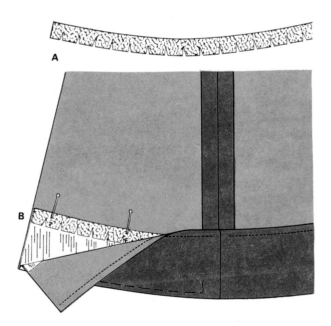

Cut shaped pieces of fusible webbing $\frac{1}{4}$ inch narrower than the measured width of the bias strip from the hem fold to the top edge. Cut enough shaped pieces of webbing for the entire length of the hem.

Working on an ironing board, with the wrong side of the skirt up, insert fusible webbing between the skirt and the bias strip [D], and **steam-press to fuse.**

[†]Numbers indicate owners of registered or trademark names, as shown on page 5.

fusibles
IN FASHION TAILORING

Tailoring a jacket or a coat can be one of the most rewarding phases of fashion sewing. Rewarding—when the garment is comfortably fitted and smoothly assembled, and has the feel and look of elegance; disappointing—when the finished product is not up to your expectations.

More than any other sewing innovation of recent years, the new fusible interfacings have inspired sewers with sufficient confidence to attempt their first tailored garments. With the advent of fusibles, they no longer have the task of shaping collars and lapels with hair canvas and padding stitches.

Experienced sewers are tailoring more garments because they no longer need to spend tedious hours making padding stitches by hand.

In some respects the use of a fusible interfacing produces results that are superior to hand-tailoring. Unlike the fabrics that are made from natural fibers, knitted or woven fabrics made of synthetic fibers are often difficult to hand-stitch. Not only do synthetic fabrics resist penetration by a sewing needle, but they also show impressions of even hidden stitches. For these reasons it is often better to use a fusible interfacing instead of a regular interfacing when you are tailoring with a synthetic fabric.

However, it is just as important to follow the traditional sewing procedures when you are tailoring with fusible interfacing as it is when you are tailoring with hair canvas and padding stitches.

The preparation steps—altering and fitting the pattern; straightening, squaring, and shrinking fabric; laying out and placing pattern pieces on the straight grain of the fabric; and cutting and marking the gar-

ment sections—are fundamental to perfectly tailored garments.

If you need to brush up on sewing and fitting procedures, refer to SINGER *Fashion Tailoring,* a book that goes into the details of fitting and altering patterns, and how to make and fit a muslin shell before cutting your fashion fabric.

Fashion Tailoring has separate chapters that show how to handle special fabrics such as plaids, stripes, and diagonals as well as sewing instructions for fur-like, leatherlike, and vinyl fabrics.

The information in *this* chapter is entirely about fusibles and how to benefit from using them in tailored garments.

There is a great deal to learn about the various fusible interfacings. There is a type, weight, and texture that is just right for any combination of fashion and fabric that you are likely to encounter. To help you choose the right interfacing, refer to the charts on pages 2, 3, 4, and 5; then, if you are still undecided, purchase several kinds of interfacing so that you can test them with scraps of your own fabric.

Also, there is much to learn about the different ways to use fusible interfacings in order to interpret a particular fashion properly.

Although the correct procedure for fusing each product is furnished with the interfacing when you buy it, such questions as how to treat interfacing for a specific effect along facing seam lines and within seam allowances, as well as many other questions, are answered in this chapter.

For tailored garments, it is good practice to simulate a part of the collar and lapel in miniature. Instead of merely fusing interfacing to a small under-collar and lapel section, go one step further and stitch a small upper-collar section to an interfaced under collar, and a small facing to an interfaced lapel. Trim, press, turn, and baste the collar and lapel edges in the same way as described in the instructions you have chosen to follow. A thorough test, such as this, will provide enough information for you to predict accurately whether the hand of the finished garment will be supple or firm.

When you plan the interfacing for a tailored jacket, the structure (woven or nonwoven) and weight of the fusible interfacing depend on how much firmness will be needed to shape the fashion, and how much support will be needed by your fabric to supply that desired firmness.

The three basic treatments that follow—firm, medium-firm, and supple—include suggested fusible interfacings and fashion fabrics that should work together to produce whatever effect you desire in your finished garment. Each treatment produces a distinctive characteristic that is different from the others.

FIRM TREATMENT OF A TAILORED JACKET

Recommended fusible interfacings: Woven interfacing, such as Fusible Acro[1] by Armo (contains hair); or woven, napped, canvas interfacing, such as Suit-Shape[3] by Stacy.[†]

Recommended fashion fabrics: Medium-weight, firm, woven and knit fabrics of wool, polyester, acrylic, and nylon, as well as blends of these and other fibers.

Special characteristics of the firm treatment:
1. Produces a crisp effect, similar to hand tailoring.
2. Interfacing extends as follows: $\frac{1}{8}$ inch into all seam allowances; $\frac{1}{2}$ inch beyond the hem folds for a soft-fold hem; to the edge of the armhole seam allowance.
3. Direction of the grain on interfacing sections is as follows:
   Under collar: place pattern arrow on the lengthwise grain of woven interfacing to obtain a bias-cut under collar.
   Jacket front: place the lengthwise arrow of the pattern on the lengthwise grain of the interfacing.
   Jacket back: place the lengthwise arrow of the pattern on the lengthwise grain of the interfacing.
   Hems: use bias-cut strips of interfacing.

Under Collar

The under collar of a tailored jacket should always be cut by a separate pattern, not by the upper-collar pattern. The interfacing should be cut by the separate under-collar pattern, which is marked for bias-cutting, and has a center-back seam. Always cut the upper collar with the lengthwise grain along a center-back fold.

When you are using woven, fusible interfacing, cut the interfacing by the under-collar pattern with the lengthwise grain line of the pattern on the lengthwise yarn of the fabric, the same way as you would cut the fashion fabric. With the wrong sides up, place the

under-collar sections of the fashion fabric on the ironing board, and steam-press.

With the fusible sides down, position the interfacing sections over the under-collar sections with the seam edges matching. Steam-press to lightly fuse the interfacing in place, but try to keep the iron away from the seam allowances so that they will not be fused securely.

Because you are going to fuse bias sections that have been cut from two different kinds of fabric, check the shape of each section with its pattern.

To make it easy to transfer the pattern markings exactly, cut two paired facing pieces out of tracing paper by the under-collar pattern. Working with one under collar section at a time, place one shaped piece of tracing paper on the interfacing, place the pattern section over it, and pin in place. With a tracing wheel, transfer the markings of the seam lines, notches, dots, and roll line to the interfacing; then remove the pins [A]. On the other under-collar section, place and pin

[†]Numbers indicate owners of registered or trademark names, as shown on page 5.

the second piece of tracing paper between the interfacing and the turned-over pattern, and transfer the pattern markings in the same way as for the first undercollar section [B].

Loosen the edges of the interfacing with your fingertips, and cut ½ inch from all interfacing seam allowances, leaving ⅛ inch to extend beyond the seam lines. To reduce bulk, cut off the interfacing diagonally across the collar points, ⅛ inch inside the seam lines.

With the interfacing side up on the ironing board, *steam-press to fuse.*

After the sections have cooled and dried, stitch the center-back seam. Press the seam allowances open, and trim to one-half width [C].

Lapel and Front

Most patterns for tailored jackets will have an interfacing pattern, but it may not be the correct one for woven, fusible interfacing. To determine whether or not the pattern is correct, place the interfacing pattern over the jacket-front pattern to see if the interfacing edges fall in the correct position for woven, fusible interfacing. If necessary, redraw the interfacing pattern.

Woven, fusible interfacing should extend to the edge of the lapel seam allowance above the bottom of the roll line, but only ⅛ inch into the seam allowances of the shoulder, front, and neckline. At the bottom, the interfacing should extend ½ inch below the hemline.

After cutting the interfacing on the lengthwise grain, use a tracing wheel and tracing paper to mark the roll line and the seam lines, except on the lapel. Transfer all other pattern markings to the wrong side of the garment sections either with tailor's tacks and hand basting, or with a tracing wheel and tracing paper.

With the wrong side up, place the jacket front on the ironing board, and steam-press to remove all wrinkles and to prevent further shrinkage.

With the fusible side down, position the interfacing against the wrong side of the front, ½ inch from the shoulder, neckline, and front edges, but with the edges matching at the armhole and lapel above the roll line [D]. Keeping the iron off the lapel between the roll line and the seam edge, and off the front, six inches above the hemline [E], *steam-press to fuse.*

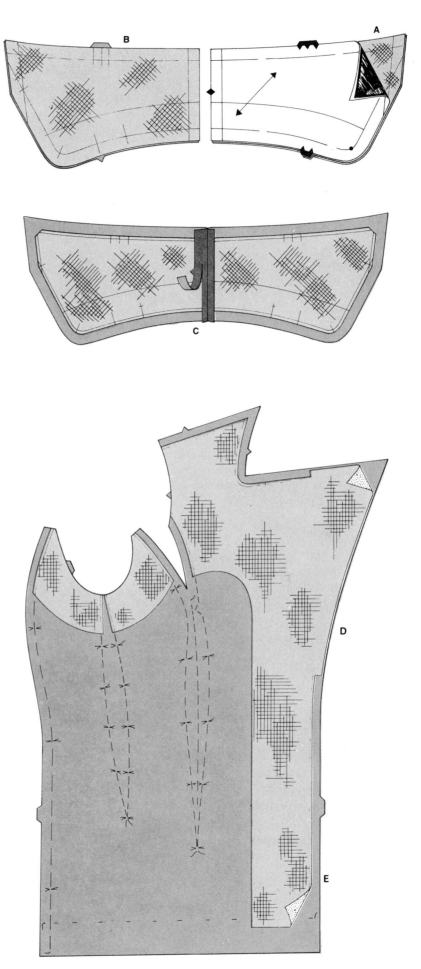

After the fabric has cooled and dried, turn the front right side up on the ironing board in preparation for fusing the lapel. Make a pad by folding a 1-inch-thick stack of newspapers in half. The folded edge of the newspapers will be rounded. Cover the pad with white muslin or sheeting to prevent the newsprint from soiling the garment. Place the pad over the garment front with the folded edge along the lapel roll line. Fold the lapel over the pad, bringing the interfacing to the top. With the flat of your hand, smooth the lapel and interfacing firmly over the roll. The seam edge of the fashion fabric will extend slightly beyond the edge of the interfacing. Except for the seam allowances, **steam-press to fuse** the lapel [F].

Measure, mark, loosen, and cut off the interfacing seam allowances $\frac{1}{2}$ inch from the edge of the lapel. Cut off the interfacing diagonally across the lapel point $\frac{1}{8}$ inch inside the seam lines. Giving special attention to the interfacing edges, **steam-press to fuse** [G].

After the section has dried thoroughly, use the pattern front to recheck the positions of the dart stitching-line markings. If there are slight variations, correct them. For interfacing the hem on the front sections, refer to *Hems* on the opposite page.

Back Shoulder Interfacing

Most patterns for tailored jackets will include a back interfacing pattern, but it may not be the correct one for woven, fusible interfacing. To determine whether or not the pattern is correct, place the interfacing pattern over the jacket-back pattern. The interfacing should extend to the edge of the armhole seam allowance [H] and $\frac{1}{8}$ inch into all other seam allowances [I]. Redraw the pattern if it does not extend into the seam allowances.

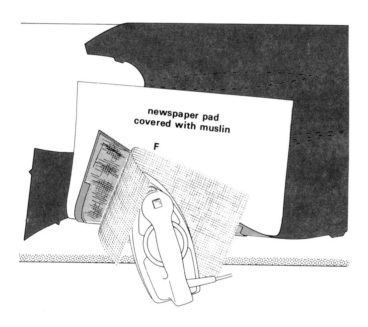

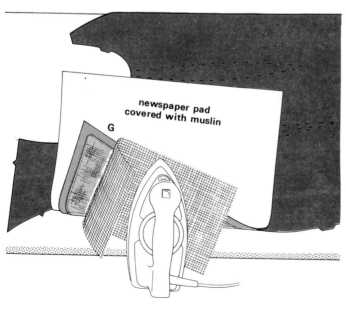

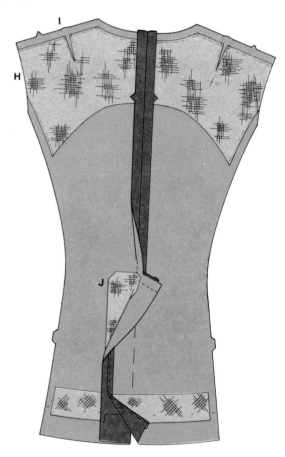

Cut the interfacing according to the grain line of the pattern. With a tracing wheel and tracing paper, mark the seam lines and dart stitching lines. On the interfacing, *slash through the center of the darts.*

While the back sections are still separate, steam-press the fabric, working on the ironing board with the jacket back wrong side up. Position the interfacing, measuring in several places from the garment edge to the interfacing seam line to position the interfacing properly. ***Steam-press to fuse.***

Instead of using fusible interfacing, some sewers prefer to use regular interfacing or underlining fabric as a stay or as reinforcement across the back shoulders. Refer to *Fashion Tailoring* or to the pattern guide sheet for the proper procedure.

Back Vent

While the back sections are still separate, mark the vent-fold lines with basting. If the length has *not* been determined, do not apply the vent and hem interfacings until the garment has been partially assembled and fitted. If the length *has been* determined, and the hem fold has been marked with basting, apply the vent and hem interfacings now.

To interface the vent, cut a 2-inch-wide bias strip of fusible interfacing for the right hand side of the vent [J], and mark a line $\frac{1}{2}$ inch from one edge of the bias strip. Position the interfacing on the right side of the vent, keeping the line-marking over the basting that marks the fold line. Allow $\frac{1}{2}$ inch of the interfacing to extend into the vent hem, and the remaining $1\frac{1}{2}$-inch width of the interfacing to extend into the garment. Position the top end of the strip at the top end of the vent, and position the bottom of the strip $\frac{1}{2}$ inch below the hemline. Do *not* interface the left-hand side of the vent. ***Steam-press to fuse.***

Hems

Interfacings for the jacket and sleeve hems may be fused in place before the jacket is assembled *only* if all fitting had been completed before the garment was cut by using a muslin shell; if the pattern was carefully pin-fitted; or if a pattern from which a jacket had been made previously is used. If you are not positive about the fitting, wait until the garment has been assembled before you fuse the interfacing to the hems.

To interface a soft-fold hem, mark the hem-fold line with basting [K]. Prepare a 2-inch-wide strip of bias-cut, woven fusible interfacing, and draw a line $\frac{1}{2}$ inch from one lengthwise edge. Place the line-marking along the hem-fold line, and allow the interfacing to extend $\frac{1}{2}$ inch into the hem. Wherever there is a vertical interfacing, such as a front or a vent interfacing, abut the hem interfacing against the vertical interfacing. Wherever there is a vertical seam, allow the interfacing to extend $\frac{1}{8}$ inch into the seam allowance, or if the garment has been assembled, allow the interfacing to extend just to the seam line. ***Steam-press to fuse.*** Refer to *hems* on pages 73 and 74.

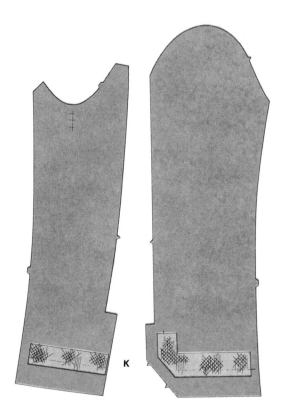

K

MEDIUM-FIRM TREATMENT OF A TAILORED JACKET

Recommended fusible interfacings: Nonwoven suit-weight that gives crosswise and has lengthwise stability, such as Stylus Fusible Uni-Stretch[1] by Armo, Tri-Dimensional Computer Dot[2] Midweight Fusible Pellon by Pellon, or Easy-Shaper[3] Suit Weight by Stacy.[†]

Recommended fashion fabrics: Woven or knit wool, wool blends, and synthetic coat and suit fabrics.

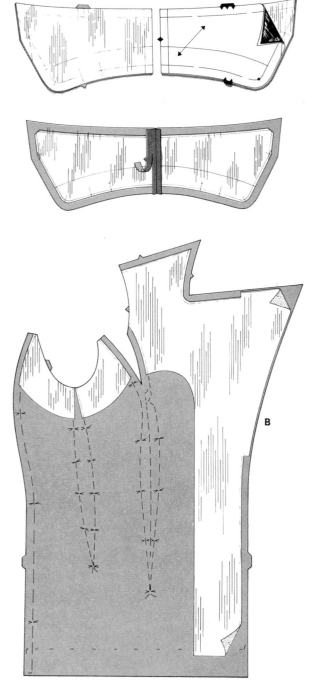

Note: Follow the same procedure for the Medium-firm Treatment that is described for the Firm Treatment beginning on page 62. The type of interfacing and the weight of the fashion fabric accounts for the difference in firmness between the two treatments.

Special characteristics of the medium-firm treatment:

1. Produces flexible shaping of all interfaced areas in medium-to-heavyweight men's and women's tailored garments.
2. The interfacing extends as follows: $\frac{1}{8}$ inch into all seam allowances; $\frac{1}{2}$ inch beyond the hem folds for soft-fold hems; to the edge of the armhole seam allowances.
3. Direction of the grain on interfacing sections is as follows:

   Under collar: place the center-back seam line on the lengthwise grain of the interfacing [A].

   Jacket front: place the lengthwise arrow of the pattern on the lengthwise grain of the interfacing [B].

   Jacket back: place the lengthwise arrow of the pattern on the lengthwise grain of the interfacing [C] and [D].

   Hems: place the lengthwise grain of the interfacing parallel to the lengthwise grain of the garment section on which the hem will be turned [E].

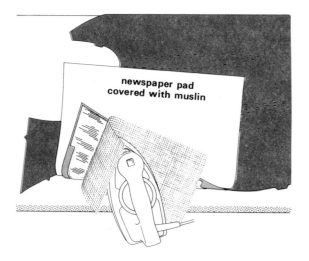

†Numbers indicate owners of registered or trademark names, as shown on page 5.

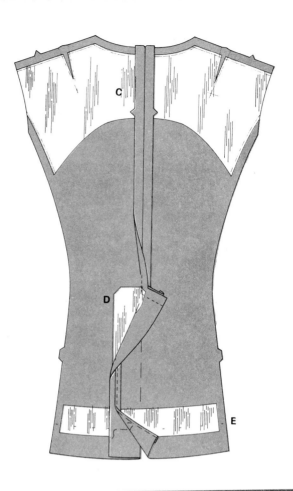

SUPPLE TREATMENT OF A TAILORED JACKET

Recommended fusible interfacings: Woven, sheer interfacing with a napped surface, such as Fusible Formite[1] by Armo. Nonwoven, lightweight interfacings with lengthwise stability and crosswise give, such as Easy-Shaper[3] Light Weight by Stacy, Stylus Fusible Uni-Stretch[1] Light Weight by Armo, and All-Bias Computer Dot[2] Featherweight Fusible Pellon by Pellon.[†]

Recommended fashion fabrics:

Lightweight, firm wovens, such as wool, blends of wool, and synthetic fibers, all-polyester, all-acrylic, tweedlike all-cotton or blends of cotton and synthetic fibers, linenlike synthetic fibers.

Lightweight, firm knits, such as nylon, polyester, or acrylic fibers, or blends of these fibers with cotton, wool, or rayon.

Special characteristics of the supple treatment:

1. Produces a soft, unstructured shaping. The degree of suppleness depends on the combination of the fabric and interfacing.

2. The interfacing extends as follows: $\frac{1}{8}$ inch into all seam allowances; $\frac{1}{2}$ inch beyond the hem folds for a soft-fold hem; to the edge of the armhole seam allowances. The lightweight interfacings used in the supple treatment are thin enough to be used to interface the upper collar and the front facing.

3. Direction of the grain for woven interfacing should be the same as indicated for the *Firm Treatment* on page 62, and for nonwoven interfacing it should be the same as indicated for the *Medium-firm Treatment* on page 66. The direction of the grain for the interfacing of the upper collar and the front facing should be the same as the fashion fabric.

†Numbers indicate owners of registered or trademark names, as shown on **page 5.**

ASSEMBLING TECHNIQUES FOR A TAILORED JACKET

The sequence in which you assemble a garment has a great deal to do with how easy it is to make. The trick is to keep bulk at a minimum. The best sequence for putting together a tailored garment that has set-in sleeves is as follows:

1. First, stitch the darts; then, either slash through the center of the dart and press it open, or press the unslashed dart in the proper direction.

Join seams within each section, forming an under collar, an upper collar, a back, a right and a left front, a right and a left sleeve, and a facing.

2. Make bound buttonholes and set-in pockets.

3. Join sections to make three separate units: the *garment unit* (do *not* stitch the side seams, but *do* attach the under collar); the *facing/upper-collar unit*; and the *sleeve units*.

4. Assemble the garment and the facing/upper-collar units.

5. Stitch the side seams of the garment, and set in the sleeves. Put in the shoulder pads.

6. Complete the hems.

7. Do all other finishing steps. Apply patch pockets. Make machine buttonholes, or finish bound buttonholes through the facing. Sew on the buttons.

8. Make the lining, and line the garment.

Garment Unit

Although pattern directions may differ slightly, essentially they all agree with this general procedure for assembling the garment unit. After the interfacing has been fused and the markings rechecked, pin, stitch, and press the darts in the back and front sections. Stitch, trim, and press the center-back seam of the under collar. Stitch and press the center-back seam of the garment. Pin, stitch, and press sectional seams, such as the side-front seam shown [A].

Make bound buttonholes and set-in pockets before joining the shoulder seams. Do not stitch underarm or side seams until after the collar and lapels have been completed so that you can work with the garment lying flat.

Stitch the shoulder seams, and press the seam allowances open [B]. Stay-stitch the neckline a scant $\frac{5}{8}$ inch from the edge, starting at the center back and stitching to one lapel dot. Overlap the stitching at the center back, and stitch to the other lapel dot. Guide the stay stitching evenly. Clip into the neckline seam allowance at $\frac{1}{2}$-inch intervals almost to the stay stitching to relieve the edges of the seam allowance [C].

Test-fitting. If you feel the need for a test-fitting, pin together the unstitched side seams, and try on the garment. If the armholes feel a little snug, remember that the armhole seam allowances at the underarm have not yet been trimmed, as they will be after the sleeves are set in.

To attach the under collar to the body of the garment, match and pin the center-back lines; match and pin the pattern dots on the under collar to the shoulder seams; and match and pin the pattern markings at each end of the neckline seam of the under collar to the markings on the lapels. When you stitch the neckline, end the stitching precisely on these markings, otherwise the upper and under layers of the collar and lapels will not match. Between these special matching points, keep the seam edges together, allowing the clips in the neckline seam allowance to spread. Baste if necessary.

With the neckline stay stitching up, stitch from the center back to the end of the neckline, just inside the stay stitching. Overlap the stitching at the center back, and backstitch, or tie the ends of the stitching at the lapel markings. Press seam allowances open over a press mitt or pressing board. Trim seam allowances to one-half width.

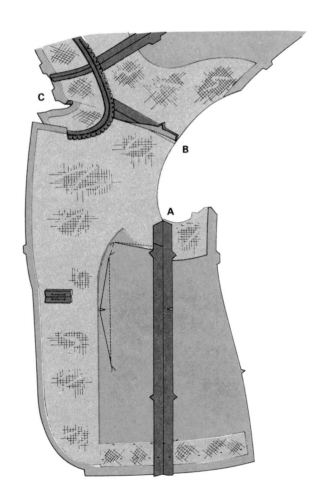

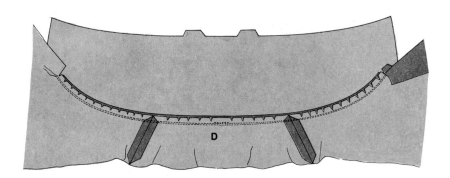

Facing/Upper-collar Unit

When you are using firm or medium-firm fusible interfacing, do not interface the upper collar and lapel facing unless the fabric is very soft or loosely constructed.

Join the shoulder seams of the back and front facings. Press the seam allowances open, and trim to one-half width.

Stay-stitch the neckline a scant $\frac{5}{8}$ inch from the edge, starting at the center back and stopping at the lapel marking. Overlap the stay stitching at the center back, and stay-stitch the other side. Clip into the neckline seam allowance at $\frac{1}{2}$-inch intervals.

First, pin the upper collar to the facing neckline at the center back; then, continue to pin, matching the pattern dots on the collar with the shoulder seams. Match the collar and lapel dots at each end of the neckline seam, and pin. If the fabric can be hand-stitched, hand-baste the collar and facing together, using short, even stitches, should basting be necessary.

Starting at the center back [D], keep the seam edges even, and machine-stitch one side of the neckline $\frac{5}{8}$ inch from the seam edge just inside the stay stitching. Backstitch exactly at the lapel and collar markings. Overlap the stitching at the center back, and stitch the other side, backstitching at the markings. Press the neckline seam allowances open, and trim to one-half width.

Sleeve Unit

The sleeve unit can be prepared either before or after the interfacing along the sleeve hem has been fused in place. Fusing the interfacing to the sleeve hem is usually done after the sleeves have been sewn into the garment because the length can then be measured more accurately. However, if you have used the pattern previously, or used a muslin shell for the fitting, the exact sleeve length will already have been established.

If the sleeve length has been determined, interface the bottom of the sleeve using 2-inch-wide bias-cut strips of woven fusible interfacing. Position the bottom of the strip $\frac{1}{2}$ inch below the marked hemline, and extend the strip $\frac{1}{8}$ inch into the seam allowances [E]. *Steam-press to fuse.*

To join the upper and under sleeve on *woven* fabrics, hold the upper sleeve right side up, and place ease stitching a scant $\frac{5}{8}$ inch from the seam edge between the notches. Pull only the bobbin thread just enough to control the slight ease in the upper sleeve. If you are using knit fabric, ease stitching is unnecessary. When you stitch, merely equalize the seam layers by holding the seam taut in front and in back of the presser foot.

Matching the seam ends and notches, pin the upper sleeve and under sleeve together at the back seam, and stitch. Backstitch at both ends. First, press the seam as stitched, then press the seam open.

To prepare the sleeve cap, place ease stitching in the upper part of the sleeve cap. Break the line of stitching at the dot marking at the top of the sleeve cap. The break in the ease stitching will eliminate ease on both sides of the marking [F].

Pin together and stitch the upper sleeve and the under sleeve at the front seam.

First, press the seam as stitched, then press the seam open. Turn the sleeve hem on the basting line, and baste about $\frac{1}{2}$ inch from the fold [G].

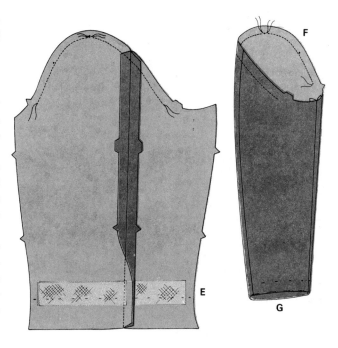

Assembling the Garment Unit and Facing/Upper-collar Unit

Assembling these units will require your most careful workmanship. Before you start, refer to the pattern pieces of the collar, under collar, facing, and the garment to verify where ease or stretch is indicated in the seam allowances. The subtle difference between the handling of one seam allowance and the other affects the shaping of the edges of the collar, lapel, or front. Because of the areas of ease and stretch, it is most important to match all pattern markings carefully, always pinning first before basting.

Stitching should be done in the direction of the arrows, as shown in [H], but do not attempt to stitch the entire seam at one time.

First, stitch the collar seam, stitching from the center back to the neckline seam with the under collar uppermost. Stop exactly at the neckline seam, draw both thread ends to one side, and tie. Overlap the stitching at the center back, and stitch the other side of the collar seam, this time allowing the seam allowances to extend in the opposite direction under the presser foot.

Next, stitch the lapel seams. With the garment side uppermost, stitch from the bottom of the roll line upward. Blunt the corner of the lapel by taking two or three stitches diagonally across the corner. Carefully join the lapel stitching with the neckline stitching, but *do not* overlap the stitching lines; instead, make two

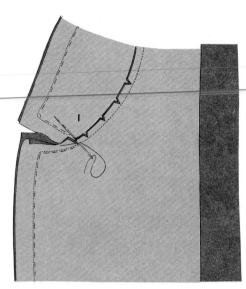

backstitches, and draw the thread ends through to the facing side. Insert a hand needle at the junction of the neckline and facing seams, and thread the needle with the thread ends. Make two hand backstitches to reinforce the seam. This gives added strength at the notch of the collar [I].

Stitch the front seams below the lapels. Stitch downward with the facing side up, and overlap the stitching.

Remove the basting, taking out short lengths one at a time. Press the seam allowances and the stitching from both sides, but do not press farther than an inch or so into the garment or collar.

Trim the seam allowances to uneven widths, keeping the widest allowance next to the side that will be

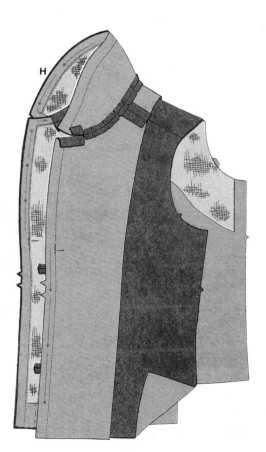

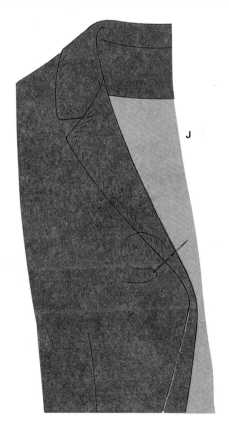

uppermost when the garment is worn. At the corners, trim lapel and collar seam allowances diagonally to reduce bulk. Notch seam allowances on curves.

Press the seam allowances open over a seam board, using steam and a moist, thin press cloth.

Turn the facing and upper collar to the right side. With your fingertips, bring the seam to the edge, but favor the side that will be uppermost when the garment is worn. Use a point turner to shape the collar and lapel corners. Hold the edges in position with diagonal basting as in [J]. Steam-press the basted edges from the underside, protecting the fabric with a moist press cloth.

Hand-understitch the seam allowances to the underside to prevent the seam that is along the edge from shifting from its basted position. Reverse sides at the roll line of the lapel. To hand-understitch an enclosed seam, use fine thread, and work from the underside near the seam. Fasten the thread end invisibly. Except for the outer layer that shows when the garment is worn, pass the needle through all layers.

Make a very short backstitch over only one yarn of the fabric, and again pass the needle through all layers, except the outer layer, for about 1/4 inch [K]. Remember to work from the side that will be underneath when the garment is worn.

Match the shoulder seams, and slip-stitch together the seam allowances of the back facing and the garment back [L].

Baste a 1/2-inch-wide strip of fusible webbing to the shoulder seam allowance of the facing [M].

Turn back the collar and lapel on the roll line, and pin through the jacket and the facing from the outside, as in [N].

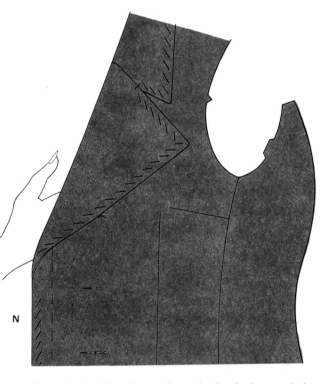

From the inside, baste through the facing and the jacket 1 1/2 inches from the edge of the facing to hold the facing in place [O]. Remove the pins.

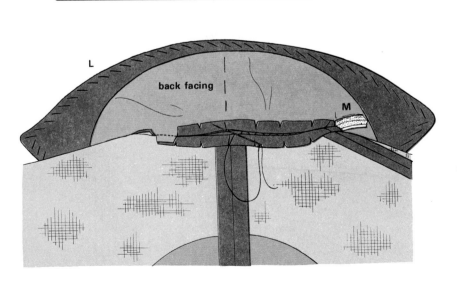

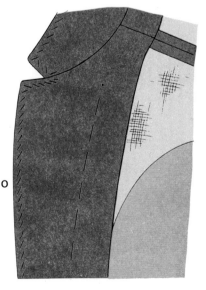

Lift the free edge of the facing, and baste a ½-inch-wide strip of fusible webbing to the inside of the facing, about ½ inch from the edge [P].

Do not fuse the facing if you intend to make bound buttonholes through the facing, or are going to sew in a machine-stitched lining. Wait until either or both of these steps have been completed before fusing the facing. Refer to pages 75 and 76.

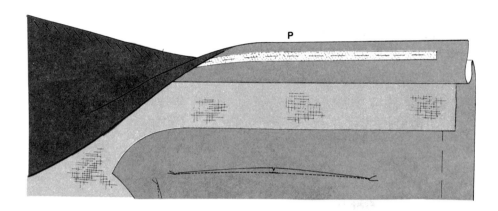

Setting Sleeves

Fusible interfacing that extends to the armhole is always included in the stitching of the armhole seam.

With the garment wrong side out and the sleeve right side out, place the sleeve into the armhole. Match and pin underarm seams or markings, notches, sleeve-top markings, and intermediate markings. Place the pins perpendicular to the seam line, nipping into the seam layers at the seam line. Draw the bobbin thread ends as much as is needed to make the sleeve fit the armhole. Distribute the ease evenly with your fingertips so that the ease will not look like gathers. Do not put ease at the top of the sleeve cap for ½ inch on each side of the marking. Pin as closely as is needed. Hand-baste with short, even basting stitches just inside the ease stitching. Remove the pins, and try on the jacket. Observe the distribution of ease in the sleeve cap and how the sleeve hangs. The armhole may feel a little snug because the full ⅝-inch seam allowance has not yet been trimmed at the underarm. When the sleeve hangs correctly, and the ease is evenly distributed, stitch the sleeve into the armhole.

When you are stitching the armhole seam, always use the straight-stitch presser foot. Stitch with the sleeve uppermost, and stitch in the direction that will place the narrow side of the presser foot on the seam allowance. Stitch just far enough inside the basting so that it will not be caught in the machine stitching. Start to stitch at the underarm, and overlap the stitching at the end. Remove the basting and ease stitching in short segments.

If the sleeve seam allowance appears to be full, hand-baste with short, even stitches ⅜ inch outside the first row of stitching to flatten the fullness. To finish the armhole seam, machine-stitch ¼ inch outside the first row of stitching. Trim the seam allowances near the second row of stitching.

Using the point of the iron from the sleeve side, press the two rows of stitching only; *do not* press the sleeve cap.

To support the roll of the sleeve cap, cut a 6-inch by 3-inch rectangle of polyester fleece or all-bias, non-woven, polyester interfacing, and pad the sleeve cap as in [Q].

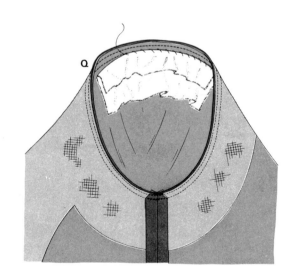

Jacket, Coat, and Sleeve Hems

Guidelines for using fusible interfacing in hems of tailored garments are as follows:

1. Cut woven fusible interfacing on the bias for hems. Abut diagonal straight-grain ends when joining strips.

2. Cut all-bias, nonwoven fusible interfacing in any direction. Abut diagonally cut ends when joining strips, but avoid joining strips as much as possible.

3. Cut nonwoven fusible interfacings that have lengthwise stability and give crosswise with the lengthwise grain running across the strip. Abut diagonally cut ends when joining strips.

4. Lightweight, nonwoven fusible interfacing is often a better choice than the medium-weight or heavyweight interfacing that was recommended in the preceding directions for collars and lapels.

5. Abut the end of a strip of fusible interfacing against the edge of a vertical interfacing; *do not* overlap the edge.

6. At crossing seams, extend the hem interfacing $\frac{1}{8}$ inch into the seam allowances, or extend the interfacing to the stitching line. *Do not* fuse a strip of interfacing over vertical seam allowances.

7. The proportions of a lined, tailored jacket determine how wide fusible interfacing should be in the hem because the edge of the interfacing will be the most prominent line of the hem. Although the interfacing can be extended either above or below the hem edge, it should not extend to the same place as the hem edge, or the line will be too prominent.

8. In a coat or an unlined jacket, the hem interfacing should be hidden by the hem. Extend the interfacing at least $\frac{1}{4}$ inch below the finished hem edge.

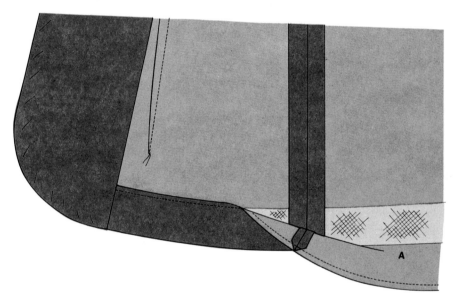

Sharp-fold hem. Extend the fusible interfacing to the fold line of the hem [A]. Abut the end of the hem interfacing against the facing edge. At crossing vertical seams, extend the interfacing to the stitching line; for an unstitched vertical seam, extend the interfacing $\frac{1}{8}$ inch into the seam allowances. Trim vertical seam allowances that cross the hem to one-half width.

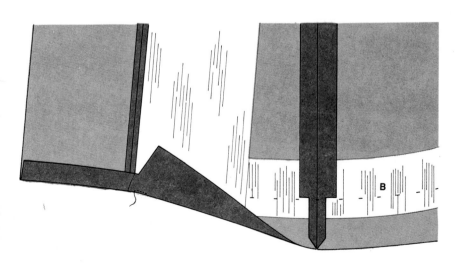

Soft-fold hem. Extend the fusible interfacing $\frac{1}{2}$ inch below the fold line of the hem [B]. Abut the end of the hem interfacing against the facing edge. At crossing vertical seams, extend the interfacing to the stitching line; for an unstitched vertical seam, extend the interfacing $\frac{1}{8}$ inch into the seam allowances. Trim vertical seam allowances that cross the hem to one-half width.

Fusing the hem of an unlined jacket or coat.
Determine the hemline by measuring the length on the wearer. Mark the hem-fold line with long basting stitches. Turn the hem up on the fold line and pin. Baste the hem ¼ inch above the fold, and press from the hem side. Trim crossing seam allowances to one-half width, clipping the basting where necessary. Measure and trim the hem to an even width. Machine-stitch ¼ inch from the hem edge. Use this stitching either to control excessive fullness in the hem edge, or merely to strengthen the hem edge. On loosely woven fabrics or fabrics that ravel excessively,

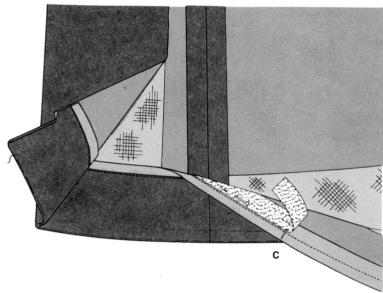

bind the hem edge with a soft, thin, bias-cut fabric or with bias, rayon seam binding [C]. On firm fabrics, finish the hem edge with machine overedging.

For either the sharp-fold or soft-fold method, apply fusible interfacing so that it extends ¼ inch below the finished hem edge.

Cut a ½-inch-wide strip of fusible webbing, and with long basting stitches, baste the fusible webbing to the inside of the hem ¼ inch below the finished hem edge.

With the hem side up, place the garment on the ironing board, and *steam-press to fuse* the hem to the interfacing.

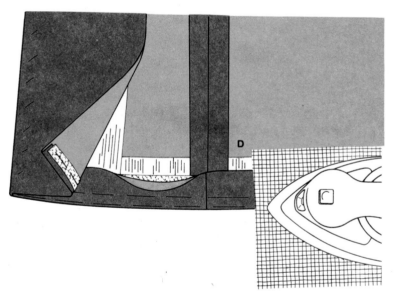

Fusing the hem of a lined jacket. Prepare the hem the same way as described above for an unlined jacket, except *do not* finish the hem edge. Interface the hem fold, using either the sharp-fold or the soft-fold method. The top edge of the interfacing may extend either above or below the top of the hem, depending on which position gives the better proportion to the garment. If you have chosen the correct weight of interfacing for your fabric, the top edge of the fused interfacing should be almost imperceptible from the outside, and only a slight hint of its width will be seen.

If the jacket hem is narrower than 1 inch, extend the interfacing above the top of the hem about ½ inch [D]. Cut a ¼-inch-wide strip of fusible webbing, and with long basting stitches, baste the webbing to the inside of the hem ¼ inch below the hem edge. *Steam-press to fuse.*

If the jacket hem is 1¾ to 2 inches wide, consider trimming the hem to 1½-inch width, and extending the interfacing ¼ inch below the top of the hem. If you do not trim the hem, extend the interfacing about ½ inch below the top of the hem.

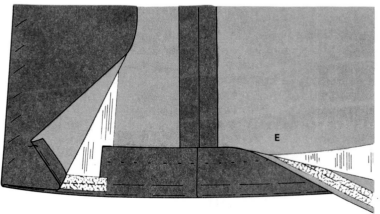

Cut a ½-inch-wide strip of fusible webbing, and with long basting stitches, baste the webbing to the inside of the hem so that the top of the webbing comes to the top of the interfacing, and not above it [E]. *Steam-press to fuse.*

FINISHING DETAILS

Bound buttonholes must be finished through the facing before a jacket or a coat is lined. Fusible webbing and fusible interfacing can be used with the windowpane and crevice-stitched methods of finishing bound buttonholes.

The windowpane method is well adapted to woven, synthetic fabrics that ravel.

Mark the buttonhole stitching lines by inserting pins straight through at the four corners of each buttonhole from the right side of the garment. Insert another set of pins in the same places from the facing side. Remove the first set of pins. Separate the facing from the garment, leaving the pins to mark the buttonhole location on the facing. Baste the outline of the buttonhole, using the pins as guides.

Cut a patch of lightweight, fusible interfacing, or cut one patch from a thin lining fabric and one patch from fusible webbing, 1¼ inches wide and 1 inch longer than the buttonhole. With the fusible side up, center the patch over the basted marking on the right side of the facing and pin. Stitch around the buttonhole marking, overlapping the stitching at the starting point. Cut through the center; then cut diagonally into each of the four corners of the rectangle. Pull the patch through to the wrong side of the facing. With your fingertips, shape the edges of the opening so that the patch does not show through the opening from the right side of the facing. *Steam-press to fuse* [A].

Center the rectangular opening over the back of the buttonhole, and baste it into place. Slip-stitch the opening to the buttonhole [B].

The crevice-stitched method is especially appropriate for knit fabrics, making use of fusible webbing to prevent raveling.

Cut a rectangular piece of fusible webbing that is 1¼ inches wide and 1 inch longer than the buttonhole. Use pins to mark the position of the buttonhole on the facing. Center the rectangular piece of webbing over the pin markings on the wrong side of the facing. Baste along the edges to hold the webbing in position; then baste the facing in position over the buttonhole.

From the right side of the garment, using the straight-stitch presser foot, a short stitch length, and matching thread, stitch in the crevice of the buttonhole seam along the edges and ends [C]. Tie the

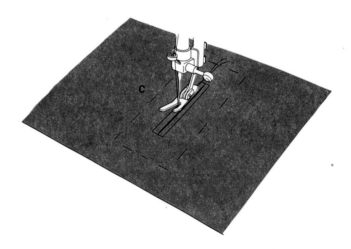

thread ends from the facing side. *Do not press yet.* Trim the facing and webbing inside the stitching lines [D]. With the facing side up on the ironing board, *steam-press to fuse.*

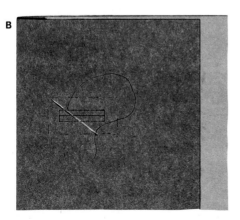

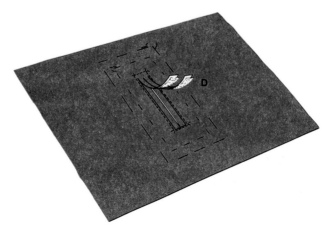

Lining a Jacket

The lining of a jacket is usually turned to the inside, and slip-stitched to the hem of the jacket, leaving a loose fold at the bottom to allow for body movement. The lining of a coat is usually hemmed separately, and secured to the coat with French tacks at the side seams.

For jackets made of knit fabrics, nylon tricot is frequently preferred to woven linings because tricot stretches crosswise with body movement. However, tricot is difficult to hand-stitch, so tricot linings are usually machine-stitched to the jacket.

To prepare a lining that is to be machine-stitched to a jacket, machine-baste the tucks and center-back fold; then join the underarm and shoulder seams of the lining and set-in sleeves.

Starting at the center back with the right side of the lining against the right side of the facing, pin and baste together the lining and facing edges. Test the fit before you stitch. If necessary, ease the lining over the bust so that the lining does not stretch while the garment is being worn. Stitch from the center back to 3 inches above the lower edge, overlapping the stitching

lines at the center back. Press the stitching.

Cut a 1/2-inch-wide strip of fusible webbing, and with long basting stitches, baste the webbing to the wrong side of the facing 1/2 inch from the stitching line. Turn the lining to the inside of the jacket, and hand-tack the sleeve and underarm seam allowances of the lining and the jacket.

With the facing side up, place one side of the jacket at a time on the ironing board, and **steam-press to fuse.** Remove any basting stitches that are visible while the fabric is still moist and warm.

Fusing the lining at the hem. Turn the bottom of the lining up to the inside between the jacket and the lining, making the fold 1/2 inch above the jacket hem fold. Baste 1/4 inch above the lining fold through both layers of the lining. Cut a 1/4- to 1/2-inch-wide strip of fusible webbing, and baste the webbing to the jacket hem where it will meet only the top edge of the lining hem, and allow for the loose fold at the bottom of the lining [E].

Steam-press to fuse. Remove any basting stitches that are visible while the fabric is still moist and warm.

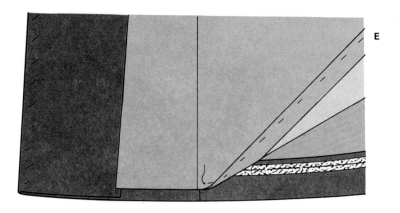

STYLING VARIATIONS OF JACKETS AND COATS

The nature of fashion is one of constant change. For a few years one style will predominate; then gradually another will take its place. As a result, to be a well-rounded sewer, it is necessary to know how to make garments that are styled in many different ways. Knowing how to handle fusible interfacing for several styles will enable you to interpret new fashions as they appear.

Princess Lines

Fusible interfacing should extend $\frac{1}{8}$ inch into princess-line seam allowances, not over the seams. Extend the interfacing $\frac{1}{8}$ inch into the shoulder, neckline, and lapel seam allowances, and $\frac{1}{2}$ inch below each hem-fold line. If the interfacing pattern is in one piece, as it would be for regular interfacing, the pattern must be redrawn for fusible interfacing as shown below.

Make the pattern for fusible interfacing by extending the front grain line upward on the pattern so that you can mark a second parallel grain line near the armhole. Lay the interfacing pattern over the garment pattern, and mark the location of the princess-line seam on the interfacing pattern. Cut apart the interfacing pattern on the marking of the princess-line seam on both the front and the back [A].

To trace the pattern, pin the interfacing pattern sections to another piece of paper, and mark new cutting lines outside the printed seam lines and outside the drawn princess lines. If the garment pattern does not include an interfacing pattern, draw lines on the garment pattern sections for the interfacing pattern, and make a two-piece pattern with one of the new pattern duplicating materials,* or use tissue paper [B].

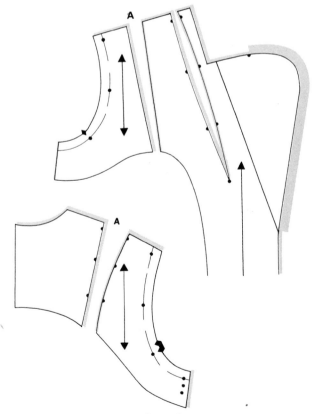

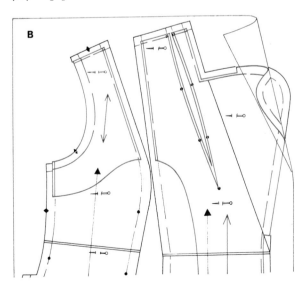

*Trace-a-Pattern by Stacy Fabrics Corporation
Kyron Kopy-rite by J. P. Stevens & Company

Shawl Collar

A jacket that has a shawl collar should be supple, not firm. Use lightweight, nonwoven fusible interfacing for a jacket; use suit-weight for a coat. Cut the interfacing for the garment front and facing on the same grain as the pattern. Because nonwoven, fusible interfacings give crosswise more than bias, cut the interfacing for the under collar with the lengthwise grain of the interfacing along the center-back seam, not on the bias, as the pattern will indicate. Extend the interfacing $\frac{1}{8}$ inch into all seam allowances. **Steam-press to fuse** the interfacing to all sections.

Although a jacket back is not likely to need interfacing, it may be necessary for a coat. Should you prefer to interface the back to prevent stretching, refer to page 64 or to SINGER *Fashion Tailoring* for instructions on applying a back reinforcement of regular interfacing or underlining fabric.

To assemble the garment unit, stitch and press the back darts and seams so that the jacket back is in one section. Stitch and press the front darts and seams, and make the bound buttonholes and pockets. Stitch, press, and then trim the center-back seam of the under collar to one-half width. Stitch and press the shoulder seams, but leave the underarm seams unstitched until the front facing is complete.

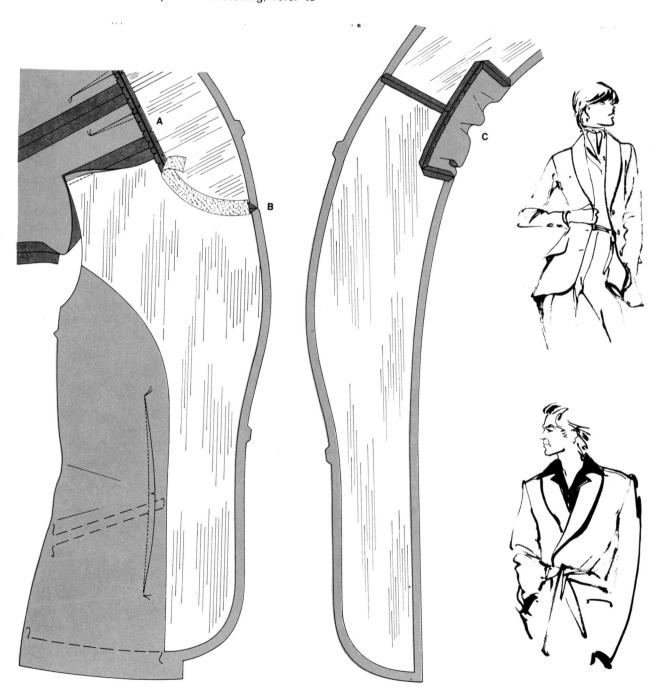

Stay-stitch the neckline a scant ⅝ inch from the edge. Clip into the seam allowances almost to the stitching. Pin, then stitch the under collar to the neckline. Press the seam allowances open, and trim to one-half width [A]. To make these seam allowances smooth so that they will not show through to the outside collar, cut a 1-inch-wide piece of fusible interfacing by the front-jacket neckline pattern. *Steam-press to fuse* the interfacing over the pressed-open seam allowances of the front neckline [B].

To assemble the facing unit, stitch the center-back seam of the collar and front facing. Press open, then trim the seam allowances to one-half width. Stay-stitch the neckline of the back facing, and clip into the seam allowances almost to the stay stitching. Stitch the back facing to the collar at the back neckline and shoulders. Press the seam allowances open, and trim to one-half width [C].

Join the garment and facing units along the front and collar edges. Trim the seam allowance of the outside layer to ¼ inch, and the seam allowance of the inside layer to ⅛ inch. Above the location for the top button, where the collar rolls back [D], trim the facing seam allowance to ¼ inch because it is a part of the outside layer. Below the location for the top buttonhole, trim the jacket-front seam allowances to ¼ inch because they have become part of the outside layer.

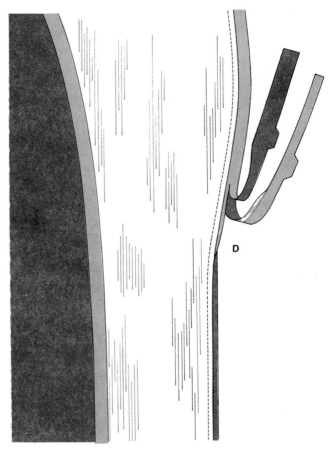

Working over a seam board, press the trimmed and notched seam allowances open. Turn the facing to the inside, and carefully form a sharply turned edge along the seam [E]. Hand-baste near the edge with diagonal basting, working the edge with your fingertips to place the seam so that it cannot be seen from the outside. Press the edge.

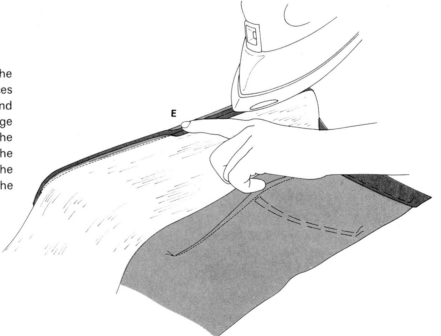

Baste the front facing of the jacket near the unstitched facing edge. Hand-stitch the neckline seam allowances of the garment and facing units together.

Complete the garment as you would any other style.

Applied Two-piece Collar

In contrast to mannish styling, dressmaker styling often calls for a two-piece collar without lapels.

Fusible interfacing that has a grain can be applied to this type of collar in either one of two ways. Apply suit-weight interfacing to the bias under collar only, using the center-back seam line as the lengthwise grain, or apply lightweight interfacing to the upper collar and under collar. Either way, apply lightweight interfacing to the garment front, and cut it on the same grain as the pattern, extending the interfacing to the edges of the seam allowances.

Interfacing the back neckline makes a better-fitting collar. If the pattern *does not* have neckline darts, cut the fusible interfacing by the facing pattern. If the pattern *does* have neckline darts, cut the fusible interfacing by the garment pattern, cutting the interfacing $\frac{1}{2}$ inch narrower than the facing on the side opposite the neckline.

Cut the back interfacing, and mark the dart and neckline seam lines with a tracing wheel and tracing paper. Trim the interfacing $\frac{1}{8}$ inch inside the dart stitching lines. Lightly fuse the back neckline facing to the wrong side of the garment, but avoid fusing the neckline seam allowance.

Lightly fuse the collar interfacings and the garment-front interfacings, but avoid fusing the seam allowances.

With a tracing wheel and tracing paper, transfer seam lines and other pattern markings to the wrong side of the fabric, or to the interfacing.

Assemble the back and front garment sections and the under collar into one unit; assemble the facing sections and upper collar into another unit.

To prepare the garment sections for assembling, work with the back section first. Stay-stitch the neckline a scant $\frac{5}{8}$ inch from the edge of the seam allowance. With your fingertips, lift the interfacing, and trim it just outside the stay stitching. Avoiding the shoulder seam allowances, **steam-press to fuse.**

Stitch and press the darts; slash and press-open wide darts, and press narrow darts toward the center back. If the back has sectional seams, stitch, and press the seam allowances open.

To prepare the front sections, stitch, and press bust darts downward; press sectional seams open, and make the buttonholes. Stay-stitch the neckline a scant $\frac{5}{8}$ inch from the seam edge. Lift the interfacing from the neckline seam allowance, and trim the interfacing. Avoiding the shoulder and front seam allowances, **steam-press to fuse.**

Join the back and front units at the shoulders. Lift the interfacing from the seam allowances and trim

outside the stitching. Press the shoulder seam allowances open. Stay-stitch across the seam allowances at the neckline.

Prepare the under collar. Lightly fuse the interfacing, and if your collar has a center-back seam, stitch the seam. Lift the interfacing from the seam allowances, and trim; then trim the seam allowances to one-half width.

To make it easier to join the under collar to the garment neckline, clip into the neckline seam allowance at evenly spaced intervals along the neckline curve, almost to the stay stitching. With your fingertips, lift the interfacing from the under collar seam allowance, and trim the interfacing close to the stitching. Press the seam allowances open, and trim to one-half width. Avoiding the outer edge of the under collar, **steam-press to fuse** the remainder of the under collar near the neckline.

To prepare the upper collar and facing unit, stitch together the front and back facings at the shoulder seams. Press the seam allowances open, and trim to one-half width. Stay-stitch the facing neckline seam a scant $\frac{5}{8}$ inch from the seam edge. Clip into the seam allowance at evenly spaced intervals along the neckline curve, almost to the stay stitching. Baste and stitch the upper collar to the neckline of the facing. With your fingertips, lift the interfacing from the seam allowance of the upper collar, and trim the interfacing seam allowance outside the stitching. Press the seam flat; then press the seam allowances open, and trim to one-half width.

Except for the outside seam allowances of the upper collar, **steam-press to fuse** the remainder of the upper collar.

Stitch the garment/under-collar unit to the facing/upper-collar unit along the collar and facing edges [A]. With your fingertips, lift the interfacing from the seam allowances, and trim the interfacing outside the stitching [B]. *Steam-press to fuse* the interfacing near the seam line.

Trim the remaining seam allowances to uneven widths of $\frac{1}{8}$ and $\frac{1}{4}$ inches, always trimming the seam allowance wider on the side that will show when the garment is worn [C].

With the garment wrong side up over a seam board, use the point of the iron to press the seam allowances open. Turn the front facing and upper collar to the right side, and favoring the side that will show the most, baste near the edges, using diagonal basting stitches. Press near the edges on both sides.

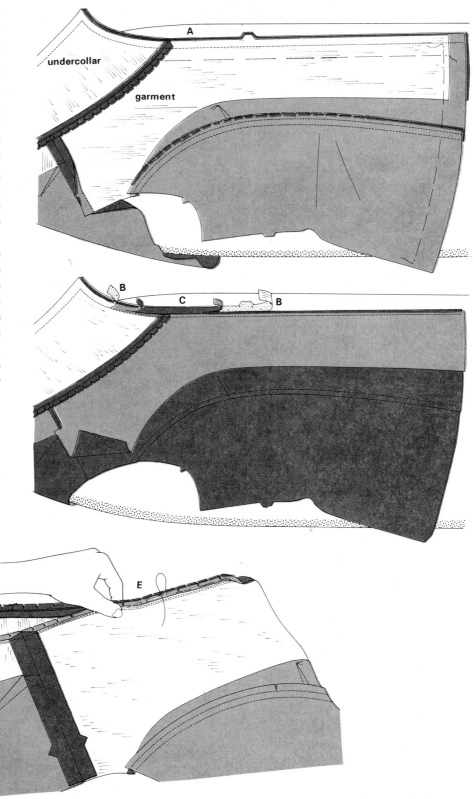

Hand-stitch together the pressed-open neckline seams, using catch stitches or slip stitches, or if your fabric is difficult to penetrate with a hand needle, stitch together the extended seam allowances, using long, plain stitches separated by short backstitches. Stitch one side with the inside of the garment up, with the collar toward you. Lay back the facing to expose the neckline seams of the upper and under collars.

Starting near the center front, stitch together the seam allowances as far as the center back [D]; then turn the garment, with the collar away from you, still keeping the wrong side up, and stitch from the other side to the center back as shown [E].

Anchor the shoulder seams of the garment and facing with fusible webbing. See [M] on illustration, page 71.

Applied One-piece Collar

A one-piece collar has a fold instead of a seam along the outside edge, and at the ends it has seams that shape the points. A one-piece collar on a jacket or a coat should be interfaced to add body and to enhance the shape, and the best place to apply fusible interfacing is on the back of the upper collar with the interfacing extending $5/8$ inch beyond the collar fold into the under collar, and $1/8$ inch into all seam allowances.

The collar fabric may be cut either on the lengthwise or crosswise grain, but the interfacing should be cut with the lengthwise grain running from end to end.

To form a crease along the outside edge, fold the collar with wrong sides together and neckline edges matching, and press. Unfold the collar, and place the interfacing on the back of the upper collar as shown [A]. The upper collar can be identified by its double notches, which match the double notches on the neckline facing of the garment front. *Steam-press to fuse.*

Transfer all pattern markings to the interfaced collar that are important in assembling the collar and attaching it to the garment. Mark the center-back collar with hand basting. Mark the pattern dots that indicate where to stop the stitching on the ends of the collar at the intersection of the stitching line and the neckline seam line. Mark the dots that indicate where the collar should meet the shoulder seam on each side.

To make a soft-fold edge along the outside of the collar, baste a $5/8$-inch-wide strip of fusible webbing to the edge of the interfacing that extends into the under collar [B]. Extend the webbing from the seam line at one end to the seam line at the other end, using machine speed-basting or hand basting.

Construct the collar unit. With right sides together, fold the collar, and stitch the ends, stopping at the pattern markings. Either backstitch or tie the thread ends. Press the seam allowances open, avoiding the fusible webbing on the edge of the interfacing. Trim the seam allowances of the upper collar to $1/4$

inch, and of the under collar to $1/8$ inch. Turn the collar right side out, and baste and press both collar ends, keeping the seam along the edge. *Steam-press to fuse* along the outside edge where the fold has been prepared previously with fusible webbing.

Cut the interfacing. On a jacket that has the front and facing cut as one, use the facing part of the front pattern to cut interfacing for the jacket front [C], extending the front edge of the interfacing $5/8$ inch beyond the front fold line [D]. Cut $1/2$ inch from all seam edges so that the interfacing will extend $1/8$ inch into all seam allowances.

If the jacket has a center-back fold, cut the interfacing by the back facing pattern. If the jacket has a center-back seam, do not place the center back interfacing pattern on a fold; instead, cut $1/8$ inch beyond the pattern fold line [E]. Trim $1/2$ inch from all other interfacing seam allowances, leaving $1/8$ inch to extend into the garment seam allowances.

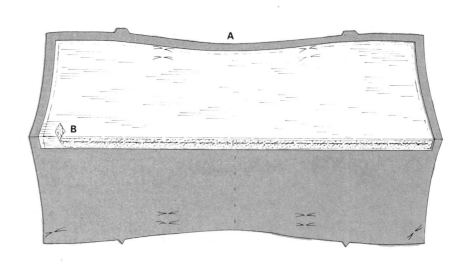

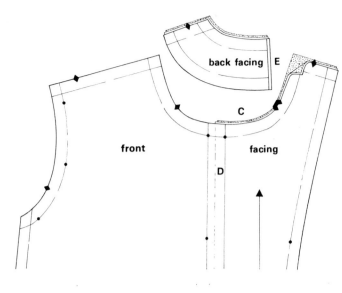

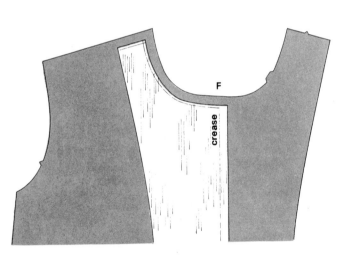

Position the front and back interfacing sections with their fusible sides against the inside of the front [F] and back [G] garment sections, as shown. *Do not interface the facings.* **Steam-press to fuse.**

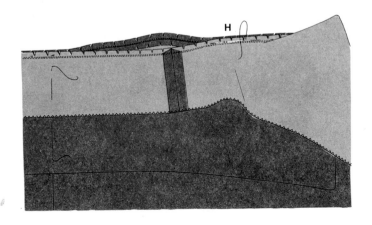

Assemble the garment unit. Make the darts in the front and back sections, and stitch and finish the center-back seam. Stitch the shoulder seams, and finish the edges of the seam allowances while the jacket is still unlined. Join the back and front facings at the shoulders; then trim the seam allowances to one-half width, and press them open.

To prepare for joining the collar unit to the garment unit, first stay-stitch the neckline of the garment; then stay-stitch the neckline of the facing a scant $\frac{5}{8}$ inch from the edge. Stitch from the center back to the front fold, overlapping the stitching each time. Guide the stay stitching accurately so that the distance from the seam edge does not vary. Clip into the neckline seam allowance at $\frac{1}{2}$-inch intervals almost to the stay stitching to allow the curved seam allowance to conform to the seam line of the collar.

Stitch the collar unit to the garment unit. Pin the interfaced upper collar to the neckline facing at the center back, shoulder seams, front neckline notches, and front fold line. Place all pins perpendicular to the seam line. Baste if you prefer; or with the stay stitching up, stitch just inside the stay stitching from the center back to the front fold, stitching on the right and left sides of the upper collar, and overlapping the stitching at the center back.

Pin the under collar to the garment neckline at the center back, shoulder seams, front neckline notches, and front fold line. Baste, or with the stay stitching up, stitch just inside the stay stitching, stitching on the right and left sides of the under collar and overlapping the stitching at the center back and at each front fold line.

Trim all seam allowances to one-half width, and press them open over a pressing board. Pin together the opened seam allowances that extend toward the garment at matching points, and hand-stitch them loosely with long, plain stitches separated by short backstitches [H]. Press the seams from both the facing/upper-collar side and the garment/under-collar side.

Cut strips of fusible webbing, and fuse together the facing and garment shoulder seam allowances; then complete the jacket in the usual way.

Covered Snap Closure

A dressmaker jacket that has been designed to be worn closed may be held in place with covered snaps. To keep the closure smooth and the snaps unnoticeable, machine speed-baste or hand-baste 5/8-inch-wide strips of fusible webbing on both fronts on each side of the center-front basting line where the snaps will be sewn.

On a jacket that has the front and facing cut as one with the interfacing extending 5/8 inch beyond the crease to form a soft fold (see illustration on the right), insert a strip of fusible webbing along the crease, and baste it in place. Baste another strip of webbing about 5/8 inch inside the center-front basting [A]. Do this for both the right and the left fronts.

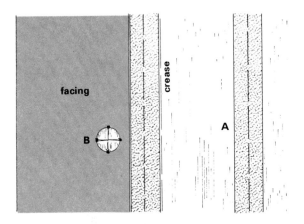

On the right-hand facing, mark the location for the ball half of the snap [B]. To reinforce the facing where the snap will be sewn, fuse a small circle of interfacing to the wrong side of the facing. Hand-stitch the snap to the facing with five or six stitches over the edge of each hole, catching the edge of the interfacing with each stitch.

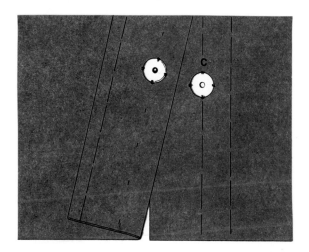

On the left-hand side of the garment layer only, center the socket half of the snap over the center-front basting line [C], and hand-stitch over the edge of each hole.

After all the snaps have been hand-stitched, place one side of the front at a time on a softly padded ironing board with the snap-side down. A soft padding, such as a bath towel, will prevent the snaps from marking the outside of the garment. **Steam-press to fuse** the right and left fronts.

Remove the basting, and press lightly to eliminate any marks that may show.

Collarless Jacket or Coat

Interface the garment the same way as you would if it had a collar, but do not interface the facing. Select the appropriate type and weight of fusible interfacing for your fabric.

For minimum support, extend the interfacing 1/8 inch into all seam allowances, except where the garment is going to be finished with topstitching; there extend the interfacing to the seam line. Make the facing 1/2 inch wider than the interfacing it will cover.

If the design of the neckline or the construction of the fabric indicates that the neckline could stretch out of shape, stay the seam with seam tape placed next to the facing. Remember to shrink and press the seam tape before you use it. For staying curves, press the seam tape into the shape of the curve while it is damp.

For shoulder support, cut the interfacing so that it extends into the armhole seam allowance as shown on page 63. If desired, interface the back also, as shown on page 64.

Raglan Sleeves

Raglan sleeves extend to the neckline, and join the back and front with bias seams. They may be cut in one piece, with a dart from the neckline to the shoulder, or in two pieces, with a continuous seam that extends from the neckline to the edge of the shoulder and down to the bottom of the sleeve. Almost any type of neckline is appropriate with raglan sleeves.

Although there are three ways to use fusible interfacing on a jacket or coat that has raglan sleeves, the collar should be interfaced in the same way that the garment would be if it had set-in sleeves. The weight of the interfacing, and the way that you use it in the body of the garment, depend on how much additional support your fabric needs to hold its shape at the shoulders and neckline.

1. For minimum support, only apply fusible interfacing to the fronts to support the closure. Stay the bias sleeve seams with seam tape or twill tape as you stitch.

2. For neckline support, interface the fronts, and apply 2-inch-wide pieces of shaped, fusible interfacing to the top of each sleeve section and to the back section.

3. For maximum shaping and support, widen the front interfacing in a curved line a little above the armhole notch [A].

Interface the top of each sleeve section to just below the shoulder curve [B]. Curve the back interfacing to extend capelike from one sleeve interfacing to the other. Shape all interfacing sections so that they join one another in a continuous curve.

Extend interfacing $\frac{1}{8}$ inch into each dart or seam allowance. If the interfacing extends a little above the armhole notches, it is not necessary to stay the bias sleeve seams.

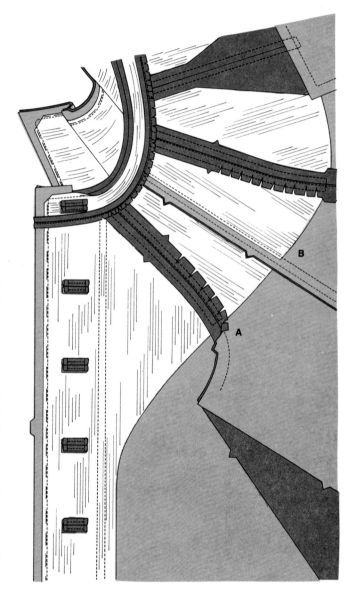

Support for top of pleat. Because the back interfacing extends to the end of the topstitching on the center-back pleat of the pants coat shown on page 85, fusible webbing can be inserted between the fold and the interfacing to support the top of the pleat invisibly, and to improve the way the pleat hangs [C]. This technique can be applied to any pleat that is backed with interfacing. *Steam-press to fuse.*

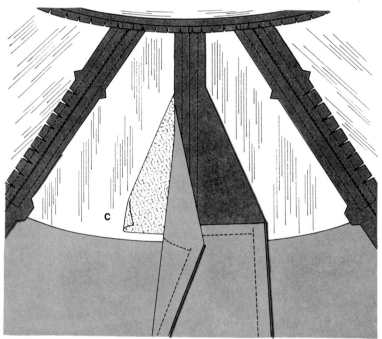

Stand-up Collar

Use medium-weight, all-bias fusible interfacing for a stand-up collar. To give added firmness to the seamed under collar, fuse a piece of shaped interfacing to the stand part as shown [D].

INDEX

A B C D E